BLACK GOLDFISH

10 KEYS TO CREATING A
DIFFERENTIATED EXPERIENCE

Stan Phelps, CSP

Published by 9 INCH Marketing
Cover by Joshua Vaughan and Layout by Amit Dey
All images from Unsplash, Pixabay, and Wikimedia Commons

ISBN: 978-1-952234-12-5

First Printing: 2022

Printed in the United States of America

Copies of *Black Goldfish* are available for bulk orders. For further details and special pricing, please email stan@purplegoldfish.com.

DEDICATION

This book is dedicated to the late marketing pioneer Theodore "Ted" Levitt.
This quote by Levitt is the cornerstone of the Goldfish Series,

"The search for meaningful distinction is central to the marketing effort.
If marketing is about anything, it is about achieving customer-getting distinction
by differentiating what you do <u>and</u> how you operate.
All else is derivative of that and only that."

ACKNOWLEDGMENTS

This book is the culmination of work I've done with 12 coauthors in the Goldfish Series. A huge thank you to Evan Carroll (*Purple 2.0* and *Blue Goldfish*), Brooks Briz (*Purple Service Edition*), Graeme Newell (*Red Goldfish*), David Rendall (*Pink Goldfish* and *Pink 2.0*), Rosaria Louwman (*Yellow Goldfish*), Brian Doyle (*Gray Goldfish*), Keith Green (*Red Nonprofit Edition*), Lauren McGhee (*Green 2.0*), Travis Carson (*Diamond Goldfish*), Tony Cooper (*Diamond Goldfish*), Alan Hoffler (*Silver Goldfish*), and Roger Burnett (*Red Promo Edition*)

TABLE OF CONTENTS

INTRODUCTION VII

SECTION I - THE WHY? 1

CHAPTER 1 - WHY A GOLDFISH? 3

CHAPTER 2 - WHY BLACK, PART ONE? 11

SECTION II - THE WHAT? 19

CHAPTER 3 - VALUE AND MAINTENANCE 21

CHAPTER 4 - WHY PURPLE? 27

CHAPTER 5 - WHY GREEN? 37

CHAPTER 6 - WHY GOLDEN? 53

CHAPTER 7 - WARMTH AND COMPETENCE 63

CHAPTER 8 - WHY RED? 67

CHAPTER 9 - WHY BLUE? 77

CHAPTER 10 - WHY PINK? 91

CHAPTER 11 - CONNECTION AND PROGRESS 105

CHAPTER 12 - WHY YELLOW? 109

CHAPTER 13 - WHY GRAY? 119

CHAPTER 14 - WHY DIAMOND? 131

CHAPTER 15 - WHY SILVER? 151

CHAPTER 16 - WHY BLACK, PART DEUX? 161

SECTION III - THE HOW? **165**

    CHAPTER 17 - I.D.E.A. FRAMEWORK.....................167

    CHAPTER 18 - FINAL WORDS...........................169

    ABOUT THE AUTHOR.................................173

INTRODUCTION

"The difference between ordinary and extraordinary is just a little extra."

- Jimmy Johnson

It all started on a rooftop…

It all started back in 2009. It was a summer evening and I was in New York City with a work colleague. Brad Bossow and I were at a trendy rooftop bar in midtown. One of those places where a bottle of beer is $15. We were waiting to meet a few people before heading over to a networking event.

This year was a pivotal one for me. I was turning 40 and I was getting introspective about work and my career. Earlier in the year, I'd created a blog called 9 INCH Marketing. Why 9 inches? Nine inches (23cm) is the average distance between the stem of your brain and the top of your heart. Given the goal of winning the hearts of your customers, I call that distance the longest and hardest nine inches in marketing. Each week I would write one or two posts exploring all facets of marketing. At the time marketing was changing rapidly. I was looking for something that could be a game-changer.

For background, I had been working for five years at Synergy. Synergy is an experiential marketing agency that created mobile tours, product launches, PR stunts, and sponsorship activations. It was the type of marketing focused on creating buzz and earned media. We'd do crazy insane activations. How crazy?

Let me share some examples:

I once helped create the World's Largest Logo for KFC. We built it near Area 51 in Nevada. The program was called *The Face from Space*. The logo was so big you could see it from space. And I know that because we shot it with the Google satellite. The program created 650 million media impressions and won awards.

I erected a 70-foot tall M&M dressed as the Statue of Liberty and floated it on a barge into the New York harbor. Right in front of Lady Liberty herself. This program was to launch a new website where you could create an avatar of yourself as an M&M.

I also once put a 40-foot Viking Ship into Times Square. This program launched all of the exclusive branded merchandise for the movie *How to Train Your Dragon* at Walmart.

At that point, I thought it couldn't get more ridiculous. But then I did the following program. I once gave away a Mediterranean Island for the brand I CAN'T BELIEVE IT'S NOT BUTTER, with none other than, wait for it ... Fabio.

These programs were successful and some even won awards. But this type of marketing wasn't scalable or sustainable.

I knew that marketing was changing...But I didn't know the way forward.

BACK TO THE ROOFTOP BAR

I noticed an older gentleman sitting across from Brad and me in the crowded bar. He was on his own for over 30 minutes and it was obvious that he was waiting for someone. Every few minutes he would scan the entire bar. I began to feel bad for him and decided to strike up a conversation about waiting. I got his attention and leaned in, "Do you know that we spend 10 percent of our life waiting?"

I told him I knew it was true because I once read it on the Internet.

We laughed and started talking about the etiquette of waiting. I stressed the importance of being on time. Right then this guy shook his head and said something I'll never forget: "There is no such thing as being on time." I protested, "Wait, I've been on time before."

He raised the pointing finger on his right hand and began shaking it back and forth like Dikembe Mutombo, "No, no, no. No one is ever just on time. You either are either early... or you are late. On-time is a myth!"

This was a complete paradigm shift for me. That night I began thinking about how this applies to business and meeting customer expectations. I've always thought that the idea of meeting expectations was a surefire recipe for losing business. It almost guarantees you will fall short. It's similar to playing prevent defense in football. Prevent defense only prevents you from doing one thing... winning.

This new paradigm has only made it clearer for me. In business, you either fall below expectations or you exceed them. There is no middle ground. It's either black or white. It bears repeating: "There is no such thing as just meeting expectations." In a world where up to 80 percent of customers describe their customer satisfaction as satisfied or very satisfied before going on to defect to other brands, simply "meeting expectations" is no longer an option.

I woke up the next morning at my home in Norwalk, Connecticut, and started thinking about companies that purposely exceeded the expectations of their customers. Companies that did the "little extra" to go beyond the transaction and honor the relationship. I decided to start a crowdsourcing effort and began a quest to find 1,001 examples.

I didn't have to go far for inspiration. Just down the hill from our house was the most profitable grocery store per square foot in the world according to the *Guinness Book of World Records*.

It's called Stew Leonard's.

STEW WHO?

Stew is a very good four-letter word. He grew up the son of a dairy farmer in Fairfield County. In the 1960s, he began working for the family business.

Clover Farms delivered milk to customers' homes. Two events would alter the trajectory of his life and the business.

The first was the decline in demand for milk delivery. Most people were now purchasing their milk at a grocery store. The second was that the family dairy farm was lost. The State of Connecticut invoked eminent domain, taking the farm to build a new highway called Route 7. Stew was forced to pivot the family business.

The result was the opening of his first dairy store in 1969.

During the first year the store was open, a couple of interactions would shape their winning approach to business.

EGGNOG AND A ROCK

The first happened two weeks after the grand opening in 1969. Stew was standing at the front door of the store greeting customers.

Suddenly a customer came up to Stew, "*YOUR EGGNOG IS SOUR!*" and thrust into his hands a half-gallon carton.

Stew was indignant, "My eggnog is sour, from my brand new dairy plant? Impossible! You're wrong! It can't be sour. We've sold over 200 half-gallons of eggnog from this batch and you're the only one who's complained!"

She snapped back, "I don't care how many cartons you sold, it's sour and I want my money back!"

Eggnog was 95 cents per half-gallon. Stew reached into his pocket and gave the customer a dollar bill.

She snatched it out of his hand and stormed out. The last words he heard her say were...

"I'm never coming back to this store again!"

That night, Stew relayed the story to his wife, Marianne. Instead of a sympathetic ear, she became visibly upset,

"I don't blame her at all," said Marianne. "You didn't listen to her. You contradicted her and practically called her a liar. I hope you are not going to run your store like other store managers, who think all customers are trying to put something over on them. They don't trust us -- but we fix them -- WE JUST NEVER GO BACK!"

After thinking about it, Stew realized that he had everything in the world tied up in the dairy store. He could not afford to lose a single customer. He realized that most customers were honest and wouldn't try to take advantage of him.

However, if he tried to protect himself from the one percent who were dishonest, he'd end up penalizing the other 99 percent who were really good and honest!

Stew decided Marianne was right and that no customer was ever going to be wrong in my store again.

On his way to work one morning, Stew drove by a monument yard in Westport. He stopped and began to watch the workers unload granite. Suddenly, Stew got an idea. He bought a huge 3-ton slab. Then Stew had the rock delivered to the front door of his store and had their stonemason chisel the store's new 2-rule policy into its face:

1. The Customer is Always Right

2. If the Customer is Ever Wrong... ReRead Rule 1

To this day, over 50 years later, the rock still stands firm at each of Stew Leonard's store entrances. And every single team member of Stew Leonard's knows the eggnog story. Employees know that they can do anything in their power to make the customer happy. Because happy customers not only come back, they bring their friends!

CAREER DAY AND WORD OF MOUTH

The second interaction for Stew was with the local elementary school principal. The principal approached him to talk about his store at an upcoming Career Day. Stew didn't really see the appeal for kids, but she pressed on and he reluctantly agreed.

That Friday morning, he drove to the school. As Stew pulled into the parking lot, he immediately knew he was in trouble.

There was a fire truck parked in front of the school with kids climbing on it. It didn't get any better when he walked in. Stew immediately saw a room with an Air Force officer showing a movie about jet airplanes.

A few classrooms down was a police officer. He was showing a packed classroom various police equipment and weapons.

Stew proceeded to walk all the way down the hall and eventually found his classroom. There was a sign on the door:

THE

MILK

BUSINESS

Stew walked into the room to find only three kids sitting inside. Two of which were the sons of his produce manager.

For the next 30 minutes, Stew talked about the dairy business. At the end, he thanked the kids. Stew then reached into his pocket and handed them each a coupon for a free ice cream at the store.

The kids left and Stew waited to present his second session. He waited and waited. No kids.

After 10 minutes, no one showed up.

After 15 minutes passed, not one kid had arrived.

After 20 minutes though, the principal came rushing in and frantically exclaimed,

"Stew, I don't know what you told those kids, but we have to move your next presentation to the school auditorium."

These simple stories underscore the power of unexpected extras and the effectiveness of word of mouth. Both events would shape Stew's thinking and approach. To this day, when you visit Stew Leonard's and buy $100 or more in groceries, you get a coupon for a free ice cream. You'll also see a three-ton rock at each store entrance.

Unless you live in New York, New Jersey, or Connecticut, you probably haven't been to Stew Leonard's. But you've probably been to a Trader Joe's. Here is the late founder Joe Coulombe on the inspiration he received from Stew Leonard's:

> I'd heard about a famous grocery in Connecticut, Stew Leonard's, who operated with only 800 SKUs. An "SKU" is a "stock keeping unit"... that means a single size of a single flavor of a single product. We'd been operating with about 6,000 SKUs available. Stew was doing 100 million in a single store ...800 SKUs...and this was 1977 so this like 180 million today...and so we adopted a 5 years plan in 1977 and we said and the end of this we will not carry anything unless we can be outstanding in it and to get there we are going to have slashed the number of SKUs down to only those products that we have such deep product knowledge that we know as

> much as the vendors. By the time I left Trader Joes we had it down to 1,100 SKUs.
>
> Was this a smart move? Trader Joe's has the best sales per square foot of any grocery store and they are one of the 100 best companies to work for in America according to *Fortune*.

THE CONUNDRUM

Merriam-Webster defines a conundrum as, "that of the seemingly unanswerable question or problem, frequently applied to heady dilemmas involving ethics, sociology, or economics."

Here's the conundrum in business. Referrals and word of mouth are the best forms of marketing. The research indicates that 85 percent of businesses say that's how customers learn about them. Sorry Google, search engines come in at a distant second at 59 percent. But even though word of mouth has such a major impact on buying behavior, less than one percent of businesses have a word-of-mouth strategy.

My initial Purple Goldfish Project sought to find examples of companies that gave "little extras" as a word-of-mouth strategy. I came across stories dating back to the 1800s. Like the story of a boy from upstate New York named David McConnell.

In 1874, at the age of 16, David started to sell books door-to-door. When his fare was not well received, McConnell resorted to offering a "little extra." David would promise a free gift in exchange for being allowed to make a sales pitch. The "little something extra" was a complimentary vial of perfume. It was a signature extra as David concocted his original scent with the aid of a local pharmacist.

McConnell quickly learned his customers adored his perfume yet remained indifferent to his books. Soon he would concentrate solely on cosmetics, starting a company called the California Perfume Company. In 1886, it would become Avon Cosmetics.

Who knew the first Avon Lady was actually a boy? Despite competition from hundreds of American and foreign brand name cosmetics today, Avon remains a leader with Avon Ladies ringing doorbells coast to coast.

And stories that spawned an entire business. Like the one about a social worker with a passion for good food and a commitment to healthy living.

In 1996, without the capital to open a restaurant, Stacy Madison and her husband began serving healthy pita bread roll-up sandwiches. Their lunch cart in Boston's Financial District became popular and soon lines started to form around the block. To make waiting more palatable (literally), Stacy concocted a little extra for customers waiting in line. Each night she would bake the leftover pita bread sprinkled with seasoning to create different flavored chips.

The chips were a huge hit with her customers. Soon Stacy's Pita Chip Company was born. Stacy's experienced rapid growth, doubling sales every year, which led to a multimillion-dollar acquisition by Frito Lay.

Collecting 1,001 examples wasn't easy. What the hell was I thinking when I came up with 1,001 examples! I should have taken the advice that someone once gave me about cross-country skiing. "If you ever think about going cross-country skiing…it's best to start with a small country." I should have picked 501 examples. It took over 27 months to finish the Project.

My first book *Purple Goldfish* came out in January 2012 and the Goldfish series was born. In the initial trilogy, *Purple Goldfish* focused on the little things you could do to improve the customer experience, *Green Goldfish* examined how to drive engagement to improve the employee experience, and the third book, *Golden Goldfish,* uncovered the importance of your "vital few" in business. Specifically, how do you do the little things to take care of your best customers and employees.

The fourth book, *Blue Goldfish,* revealed how to leverage technology, data, and analytics to improve the customer experience. Blue was a reference to a tenth-century Danish king. Blue represents the convergence of big data and little data coming together to deliver high-level personalized experiences.

In the fifth color, *Red Goldfish* explored how being "for purpose" drives happiness and adds a sense of meaning for customers, employees, and society. Red was inspired by the lead singer of the band U2.

In the sixth color, *Pink Goldfish* returned to the marketing roots of Purple. It examined differentiation and how to create competitive separation in business. The idea that your flaws hold the keys to what makes you awesome. Pink was inspired by my co-author David Rendall.

The seventh color was Yellow. *Yellow Goldfish* looked at how companies can do a little extra to contribute to the happiness of their customers, employees, and society. Yellow was inspired by the warmth of the sun and a design created by Harvey Ball.

The eighth color was Gray. *Gray Goldfish* examined how to navigate the gray areas of leading five different generations in the workforce. It is no longer a "one-size-fits-all" leadership proposition.

The ninth color was literally a gem. The *Diamond Goldfish* was about sales and client management. It explored how to excel under pressure and operate via the Diamond Rule in business. The use of Diamond was inspired by how the gem is created. To quote Henry Kissinger, "A diamond is a chunk of coal that did well under pressure."

That brings us to silver. The 10th color, *Silver Goldfish*, explores the keys to coming across "Loud" and "Clear" when communicating. Specifically, addressing how to rise above distractions when presenting and how to craft content with clarity in a way that makes your message memorable.

A decade, many colors, metals, and one gem. I'm excited to share *Black Goldfish*. Black is the culmination of what I've learned over the last 10 years about DX. DX is achieved by creating a differentiated experience.

The one constant in the Series is the metaphor of a Goldfish. Why a Goldfish? Let's find out.

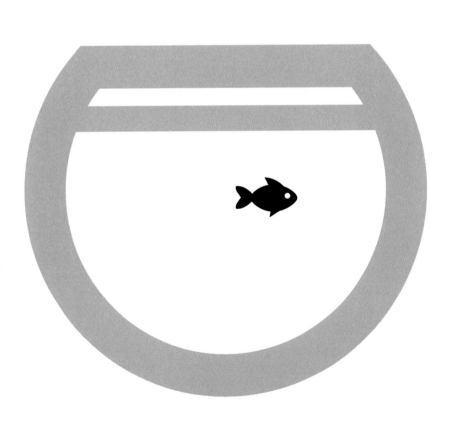

SECTION I

THE WHY?

CHAPTER 1

WHY A GOLDFISH?

"It has long been an axiom of mine that the little things are infinitely the most important."
– Sir Arthur Conan Doyle

The Goldfish in the Goldfish Series of books is a metaphor. A metaphor for growth via a differentiated experience (DX). But, why a Goldfish?

Kimpton Hotels is one part of the inspiration. Kimpton gets the guest experience. The hotel chain has a number of signature extras that go above and beyond expectations for customers. If you stay at a Kimpton, there is always free gourmet coffee in the lobby. There is fresh fruit and in the afternoon the hotel does wine tasting. Not samples—full glasses of wine.

Some Kimpton Hotels will let you take out a bike for free to tour the city. All Kimptons are pet-friendly. Bring your dog for free and they'll treat your pup like royalty. My favorite "little extra" was introduced by Kimpton all the way back in 2001.

Perhaps you were staying at a Kimpton and getting a little lonely. Perhaps you and your family are away from home and missing your family pet. To counter this, Kimpton created a program called Guppy Love.

It offers guests the ability to adopt a temporary travel companion for their stay—a goldfish. This signature program gained the hotel chain national attention. Steve Pinetti, Senior Vice President of Sales & Marketing for Kimpton shared this about the program, "[It] is a fun extension of our pet-friendly nature as well as our emphasis on indulging the senses to heighten the travel experience…'Guppy Love' offers one more unique way to relax, indulge and promote the health of mind, body, and spirit in our home-away-from-home atmosphere."

Imagine having a pet goldfish for your stay? Is there any chance you are not posting about the experience online or telling your friends and coworkers about the experience? NONE.

The other reason behind the metaphor of a goldfish has to do with my childhood.

At age six, my first pet was a goldfish. His name was Oscar. I won him at a Spring Fair by throwing a ping pong ball in a carnival game. Oscar was small, maybe an inch (2.5 cm) in length. It turns out that the average goldfish is just over three inches (8 cm). That's the length of your thumb. Yet the largest in the world is just under 19 inches (47 cm). That's the length of the average domesticated house cat.

GUINNESS WORLD RECORD GOLDFISH

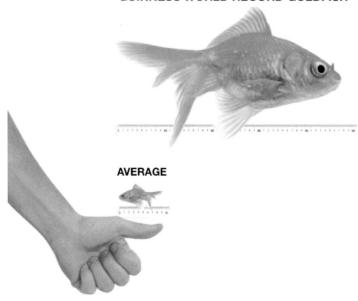

AVERAGE

We're not talking about a carp or a koi, but an ordinary goldfish. That's more than five times the average size. To put that into perspective, imagine walking down the street and bumping into someone 30 feet (9 meters) tall.

How can there be such a disparity between a garden variety goldfish and their monster cousins?

It turns out that the growth of the goldfish is determined by five factors. And those same five factors also directly relate to the growth of any business.

Let's unpack the five factors:

#1. The first growth factor for a goldfish is the **SIZE OF THE ENVIRONMENT** they are in. Most people are familiar with this growth factor. The size of the bowl or pond is one determinant of how much they will grow. The size is a direct correlation. The larger the bowl or pond, the larger the goldfish can grow.

The same reasoning applies in business. The smaller the market for your product or service, the lesser the growth. In business, what's the equivalent of the bowl or the pond? It's simply the **MARKET** for your product or service.

Takeaway: The bigger the market, the more you can grow.

FACT- The current *Guinness Book of World Records* holder for the largest goldfish hails from The Netherlands at a whopping 19 inches (50 centimeters).

#2. The second growth factor for a goldfish is the **NUMBER OF OTHER GOLDFISH** in the environment. This is an inverse correlation. The more goldfish in the bowl or pond, typically the less growth achieved. With fewer goldfish, the more they grow.

Who are the other goldfish in business? This answer is simple. They are your **COMPETITION**

Takeaway: The more competition, the harder it is to grow. The less competition, the easier it is to grow.

#3. The third growth factor is the **QUALITY OF THE WATER** that the goldfish is in. Nutrients and cloudiness in the water will impact the growth of a goldfish. The better the quality—the more nutrients and less cloudiness in the water—the more growth. Conversely, fewer nutrients and more cloudiness will hamper growth.

What is the equivalent of the quality of water in business? Here we need to think in a macro and environmental sense. The quality of the water is the **ECONOMY**. It is a direct correlation.

Takeaway: The better the quality of the economy and the greater consumer confidence, the larger the growth. The weaker the economy or capital markets, the more difficult it is to access capital and grow.

FACT - A malnourished goldfish in a crowded, cloudy environment may only grow to two inches (five centimeters).

#4. The fourth factor for a goldfish is how they're treated in the **FIRST 120 DAYS** of life. The nourishment and treatment they receive as babies are key to their future growth. Goldfish are tiny when they are born. They typically have up to one hundred brothers and sisters. They are about the size of the head of a pin. What do you call a baby goldfish? A baby goldfish is a fry. Now you know where the term "small fry" comes from. The lower the quality of the food and treatment as a fry, the more the goldfish will be stunted for future growth.

What's the equivalent of the first 120 days in business? A business is typically called a **START-UP** during its early days in business.

Takeaway: How a start-up does in the first four months of its existence will be a determining factor of how it will do in the long term.

#5. The fifth and final growth factor for a goldfish is **GENETIC MAKEUP**. The strength of its genetics will determine future growth. The stronger its genes and the more it is separated from the rest of the goldfish, the more it typically grows. The poorer the genes and the more it hangs out in the same goldfish group, the less it will grow.

What's the equivalent of genetic makeup in business? It is **DIFFERENTIATION**.

Takeaway: The more differentiated the product or service from the competition, the better the chance for growth. The less differentiated and the more a business is like the competition, the harder it will be to grow.

WHICH OF THE FIVE FACTORS CAN YOU CONTROL?

Let's assume you have an existing product or service and have been in business for more than four months. Which of the remaining four factors do you have control over?

1. Size of the bowl = Market

2. Number of other goldfish = Competition

3. Quality of water = Economy

4. Genetic makeup = Differentiation

Do you have any control over the market, your competition, or the economy?

NO, NO, and NO.

The only thing you have control over is your business's genetic make-up or how you differentiate your product or service. And how are you going to differentiate? What's the number one thing you are going to compete on?

Research by Gartner shared that 89 percent of companies believe that the number one thing they'll compete on is the experience they provide. It's no longer price, location, or even service. It's the entire experience. Gartner asked the same question in 2011. Only 36 percent of companies elected experience as the number one factor. That provides stark evidence on how much more important the experience is today. In fact, 86 percent of buyers are willing to pay more for a great customer experience.

If a goldfish is a metaphor for growth through differentiation, then what is up with all the colors? And why is this the Black version?

CHAPTER 2

WHY BLACK?

"But when I fell in love with black, it contained all color.
It wasn't a negation of color. It was an acceptance.
Because black encompasses all colors.
Black is the most aristocratic color of all....
You can be quiet and it contains the whole thing."

— Louise Berliawsky Nevelson

Why black in *Black Goldfish*? It's black for the simple reason that you get black when you combine all of the other colors in the spectrum.

For example, when you combine the three primary colors of red, green, and blue you get...

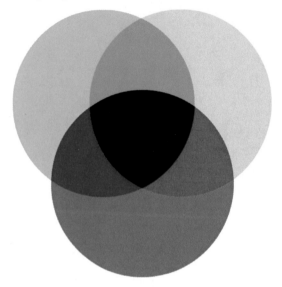

Or have you ever watched a toddler with a variety of paint colors? Eventually, they all get mixed together. And when they do, guess what? You got it, you get black.

For this book, black is an amalgam of the first 10 colors in the Goldfish Series. The black in *Black Goldfish* happens when you put all the other colors together. Here's a quick overview of all 10 colors:

PURPLE - little things that add value or make it easier for customers

GREEN - little things that drive engagement and reinforce culture for employees

GOLDEN - little things for your "vital few" employees and customers

BLUE - leveraging technology, data, and analytics to improve customer experience

RED - embracing purpose in business to benefit employees, customers, and shareholders

PINK - differentiating by defying normal and exploiting imperfection

YELLOW - contributing to the happiness of customers, employees, and society

DIAMOND - excelling under pressure in sales and client management

GRAY - leading across the five generations in the modern workplace

SILVER - rising above distractions to communicate both loud and clear

ENTER THE BLACK MATRIX

Technically, you can't write a business book without having a matrix. Not a law perhaps, more like an unwritten rule. Most matrices are 2 by 2. We are going to take it "one louder" in *Black Goldfish* with a 3 by 3 matrix.

Let's breakdown our Black Matrix starting with the vertical Y-axis:

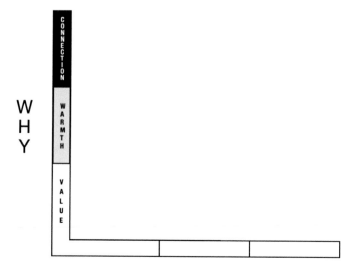

The Y-axis (no pun intended) represents the "WHY" of business. It is the purpose or intent of your product or service. To steal a French saying, it is your raison d'être. It starts with value at the foundation, levels up to warmth, and graduates to connection at the highest level.

Now, let's tackle the horizontal X-axis.

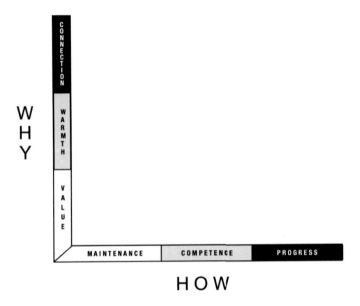

The X-axis is the "HOW" in business. It represents the experience you provide to customers and the impact on their lives. The HOW starts with maintenance (ease of doing business), levels up to competence, and graduates to progress.

A COLORFUL STORY OF THE BLACKEST BLACK

To be clear, there is black and there is Vantablack. Vantablack was created by UK-based Surrey NanoSystems in 2014.

The scientific explanation of how they made something so black and why it looks so black is confusing and technical. So much so that I'm going to just skip over the explanation. But trust me, it's really, really, really black. When you look at vertically aligned nanotube arrays, it's like looking into a void. A 3-D object coated in Vantablack looks two-dimensionally flat.

Anish Kapoor, a very famous artist, negotiated for the exclusive rights to use Vantablack for artistic purposes. The exclusivity of the license means that no other artist can use it without his permission.

Nobody.

Ever.

You probably haven't heard of Anish Kapoor, but you would recognize his work. For example, he designed *Cloud Gate*. *Cloud Gate* is better known as "*The Bean*" in Chicago. You've probably seen it. It's coated in reflective chrome.

You almost certainly haven't heard of Stuart Semple. He is a relatively unknown artist.

Stuart found out about Vantablack from his mom and was outraged that no other artists had access to it. So he decided to fight back. Stuart created the Pinkest Pink paint and began selling it under one condition. Anyone can buy it, except for... Anish Kapoor. Anyone who purchases it must agree to the following statement on his website:

> By adding this product to your cart you confirm that you are not Anish Kapoor, you are in no way affiliated to Anish Kapoor, you are not purchasing this item on behalf of Anish Kapoor or an associate of Anish Kapoor. To the best of your knowledge, information, and belief this paint will not make its way into the hands of Anish Kapoor.

Semple didn't expect to sell a lot of pink, he was just trying to make a point. But the demand for pinkest pink was huge and he was nearly overwhelmed filling the avalanche of orders. He ended up enlisting family members to help.

Of course, Anish Kapoor eventually got his hands on the pinkest pink. He dipped his middle finger in it and posted a photo on *Instagram.*

Chalk one up for Anish. But Semple had made his point and had galvanized the art community against Kapoor and his selfish Vantablack hoarding. He also became much more well-known in the process.

FACT

Vantablack is no longer the blackest black. In 2019, MIT developed a black material which absorbs 99.995% of light. Sorry, Anish.

He used his new popularity to engage other artists in an effort to create an affordable and accessible black that would be nearly as good as Vantablack. He created Black 1.0, sent hundreds of samples out, and asked people to try to make it blacker. They did and the result was Black 2.0. Black 3.0 launched in 2019.

The bottom-left level of the Black Matrix deals with the concepts of value and maintenance for customers. Let's look at both next.

SECTION II

THE WHAT?

CHAPTER 3

VALUE AND MAINTENANCE

"I like to be stylish and edgy, but also low maintenance."

— Krysten Ritter

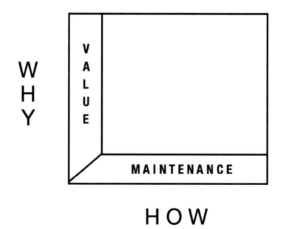

When I was single, I had two qualifiers that helped guide my dating philosophy. Back in college, I called them "value" and "maintenance." A prospective date was rated on both scales. Value represented "fun to be with" and maintenance dealt with "effort needed to maintain the relationship." The ideal in my college days was high value and low maintenance.

Note: if you don't understand what maintenance is, that means you're probably HIGH MAINTENANCE.

I believe these same two factors of value and experience apply to customer experience.

First, let's define customer experience. I ascribe to the definition of customer experience (CX) shared by friend and fellow speaker Mike Wittenstein.

Mike sees CX as the following equation:

> Everything that your product or service does for your customers (Value)
>
> - Minus everything that your business processes do to your customers (Maintenance)
>
> _____
>
> = The result of the equation is how the experience makes your customer feel (and more importantly what they tell others about that experience)

Let's explore both concepts starting with VALUE:

In business, price represents what you pay. And price is only relevant to the value received. Value is what you get. Value is crucial in terms of both differentiation and word of mouth. To quote legendary marketer Seth Godin, "The thing that makes something remarkable isn't usually directly related to the original purpose of the product or service. It's the extra stuff, the stylish bonus, the design or the remarkable service or pricing that makes people talk about it and spread the word."

VALUE represents the "what" and "why" of experience. Here are the elements of value:

- Beyond the product or service, what are the tangible and intangible benefits that you receive?

- Did the brand go above and beyond to exceed expectations to honor the relationship?

- Did the brand give that little unexpected extra to surprise and delight?

Now, let's tackle MAINTENANCE:

Maintenance is the "who" and "how" of experience:

- What is the onboarding or buying experience like?

- Does the brand make things turnkey or simple?

- Are they responsive to problems/issues?

At the end of the day, you take all the value received and weigh it against the business processes you were subjected to. In our on-demand world, the effort you have to expend can dramatically impact the experience.

Both value and maintenance are represented below in the Value Maintenance (VM) Matrix.

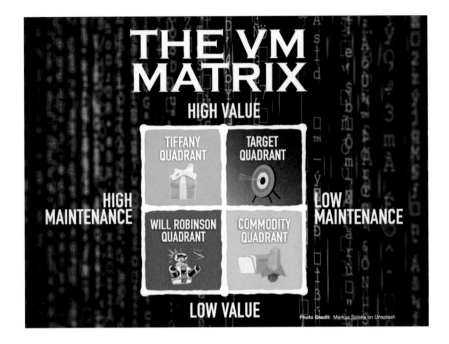

The VM Matrix is composed of four quadrants. The goal is to be seen as high value and low maintenance. Let's examine the matrix starting clockwise from the bottom right:

Commodity Quadrant - Brands here lag in a sea of sameness. They provide low value, but they are relatively easy to work with. The challenge here is price. It becomes one of the only differentiators. And unfortunately, that becomes a race to the bloody red bottom.

Will Robinson Quadrant - Brands here are in grave danger. Providing low value and being difficult to do business with is a recipe for disaster. Listen to the *Lost in Space* robot, "Danger, danger, danger Will Robinson."

Tiffany Quadrant - Brands here provide a ton of value, but they are high maintenance. You can survive here, but it is precarious. Some people will justify the effort because of the value. For them "the juice is worth the squeeze." But for most customers, they'll kick these brands to the curb for being difficult to work with.

Target Quadrant - The top right is the ideal target for brands. You want to be perceived as providing high value. And you are easy to work with, especially if any issues arise.

The combination of value and maintenance nets out to be about a feeling. Because a brand today is no longer just what you tell people it is. It's the differentiation that the customer experiences, it's how they FEEL about that experience, and most importantly... what they tell others about their experience.

Value and maintenance begin with the first color in the Goldfish Series. Let's look at why the color purple in *Purple Goldfish*.

CHAPTER 4

WHY PURPLE?

"We picked up one excellent word–
a word worth traveling to New Orleans to get;
a nice limber, expressive, handy word– 'lagniappe.'"

- Mark Twain

Purple was the first color in the Goldfish Series in 2012.

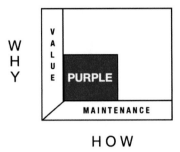

Why Purple? It was an ode to New Orleans and its most famous event. That event is Mardi Gras.

Purple is an homage to Mardi Gras because there is one word that comes from New Orleans that epitomizes the need to exceed customer expectations. That word is lagniappe. It is a Creole word meaning "the gift" or "to give more." Pronounced *lan-yap*, the practice originated in Louisiana in the 1840s. It was commonplace for a merchant to give a customer a little something extra at the time of purchase. It is a signature personal touch by the business that creates goodwill and promotes word of mouth.

Here is the definition according to *Webster's*:

LAGNIAPPE (lan'y p, lăn-yăp') Chiefly Southern Louisiana & Mississippi

1. A small gift presented by a store owner to a customer with the customer's purchase.

2. An extra or unexpected gift or benefit.

INTERESTING FACT

Napa comes from yapa, which means "additional gift" in the South American Indian language, Quechua, from the verb yapay "to give more."

Mark Twain was so smitten by the word "lagniappe" that he wrote about it in his autobiography *Life on the Mississippi*:

> We picked up one excellent word–a word worth traveling to New Orleans to get; a nice limber, expressive, handy word– "lagniappe."

> They pronounce it lanny-yap. It is Spanish– so they said. We discovered it at the head of a column of odds and ends in the Picayune [newspaper] the first day; heard twenty people use it the second; inquired what it meant the third; adopted it and got facility in swinging it the fourth. It has a restricted meaning, but I think the people spread it out a little when they choose. It is the equivalent of the thirteenth roll in a baker's dozen. It is something thrown in, gratis, for good measure.

> The custom originated in the Spanish quarter of the city. When a child or a servant buys something in a shop–or even the mayor or the governor, for aught I know–he finishes the operation by saying– 'Give me something for lagniappe.' The shopman always responds; gives the child a bit of licorice root, gives the servant a cheap cigar or a spool of thread.

Purple represents any time a business purposely goes above and beyond to provide a little something extra. It's a marketing investment back into your customer base. It's that unexpected surprise that's thrown in for good measure to achieve product differentiation, drive retention, and promote word of mouth.

After my rooftop moment-of-truth in 2009, I began my quest to find 1,001 examples of lagniappe in business. When looking across hundreds of crowdsourced examples, patterns began to emerge. It took over 27 months to reach 1,001 examples. What I found were 10 different types of Purple Goldfish. Five reside in the category of value and five in the category of maintenance.

Here is an overview of the 10 types of Purple Goldfish:

#1. Throw-ins (value) – little extras that are included with your product or service. Something thrown-in for good measure. They help you stand out in a sea of sameness.

Examples: Southwest Airlines offers "Bags Fly Free" and no change/cancellation fees. Doubletree Hotels provides you with a warm chocolate chip cookie when you check in.

#2. Sampling (value) - an additional taste by offering a free something extra on the house.

Examples: Order a box of tea from Bigelow and you'll be treated to a sample of another flavor. Order a scoop of ice cream at Izzy's Ice Cream and you get to pick a mini-scoop of another flavor for free.

#3. First & Last Impressions (value) - you have two chances to make an impression. When your customer comes through the door and right before they walk out, hang up, or log off. These little extras make you memorable and more importantly talk-able.

Examples: When you check in the Hard Rock Hotel, they'll let you sample a Gibson guitar. Moe's Southwest Grill is known for its signature welcome, *"Welcome to Moe's!"*

#4. Guarantees (value) - giving your customers that little extra pledge that you'll stand behind your product or service.

Examples: Zappos gives customers one year period to return products. Hampton Inn has a satisfaction guarantee, "If you're not 100 percent satisfied, we don't expect you to pay."

#5. Pay it Forward (value) - giving a little extra back to the community.

Examples: If you are out of work and need a suit cleaned for an interview, Plaza Cleaners will clean it for free. TOMS matches every pair of shoes purchased with a new pair of shoes for a child in need.

#6. Follow Up / Thank You (maintenance) - little extras to follow up with your customer and/or to say thank you.

Examples: Rite Aid follows up with a call to check on a patient. Mitchell's writes five handwritten notes per day to thank customers.

#7. Added Service (maintenance) - the little extra that's an added unexpected service.

Examples: Safelite repairs or replaces your glass, but they also vacuum your car and clean your windows. Call Zappos and if they do not have the shoes you want in stock, they will actually recommend a nearby store that does.

#8. Convenience (maintenance) - the little extras you add to make things easier for your customers.

Examples: TD Bank is open 7 days a week and some nights until 8 p.m. Sport Clips uses its website and mobile apps to allow customers to see the wait time at all nearby locations.

#9. Waiting (maintenance) - all customers hate to wait. If it's inevitable, how can you do a little extra to make it more bearable?

Examples: While you wait for your table, enjoy a glass of wine on the house from the Pacific Cafe. Free peanuts while you wait for your meal at Five Guys Burgers & Fries.

#10. Handling Mistakes (maintenance) - admitting that you're wrong and doing the little extra above and beyond to make it more than right.

Example: Nurse Next Door - this nursing agency in Canada takes the idea of "humble pie" to heart, literally delivering a pie when they make a mistake.

PURPLE GOLDFISH STRATEGY

Purple Goldfish Strategy is differentiation by added value. Finding signature elements that help you stand out, improve customer experience, and drive positive word of mouth. They are little consistent extras that either add value or reduce the effort for customers.

CAN A LITTLE EXTRA MAKE A HUGE DIFFERENCE?

Years ago an experiment was conducted at a restaurant. The researchers wanted to determine the effects of doing a little extra. The extras included a small gift and a greeting upon entry to the restaurant. Two types of gifts were used. Customers received either a small sample of yogurt or an inexpensive key chain.

Hershey H. Friedman and Ahmed Rahman aimed to study the impact of greetings and gifting on how much was spent, on the performance rating, and on how strongly the establishment was recommended.

The experiment studied four groups:

1. The Control Group - These customers didn't receive either a greeting or a gift.

2. The Greeting Group - These customers received a greeting, but not a gift.

3. The Gifting Group - These customers received a gift (either a yogurt sample or key chain), but not a greeting.

4. The Greeting and Gifting Group - These customers received both a gift and a greeting upon entering the restaurant.

The study looked at the impact on subsequent purchases, the greeting and gifting experiment took place before the purchase. The study could measure the impact on same-day sales. What was the impact? Here are the eye-opening results:

1. **The Control Group** average purchase was $7.11 (These customers received neither a greeting nor a gift.)

2. **The Greeting Group** average purchase was $8.39 (These customers received only a greeting)

3. **The Gifting Group** average purchase was $9.39 (These customers only received a yogurt sample or a key chain)

4. **The Greeting and Gifting Group** average purchase was $10.41 (These customers received both a gift and a greeting upon entering the restaurant.)

The difference in the amount spent between the group that was not greeted or given a gift ($7.11) and the group that was greeted and given a gift ($10.41) was a 46.4 percent increase, a considerable amount.

It is important to note that the greeting and the gifting weren't over the top. Guests were greeted with, "Thank you for choosing [name of restaurant]. Here is a token of our appreciation." Then they were presented with their gift. The gifts were basic. The key chain was a generic branded product that was not sold or advertised by the restaurant and retailed for about 40 cents. The yogurt samples were the same Dannon Light and Fit yogurt cups advertised and sold by the restaurant and retailed for about 50 cents.

The study reinforces the power of a Purple Goldfish based on the underlying principle of reciprocity. Robert Cialdini shared the concept in his book, *Influence*, "Reciprocity is based on the idea that people who receive a gift or benefit from someone have the need to give something back in return; there is actually a feeling of indebtedness on the part of the recipient." This surplus creates an obligation and implicit expectation of return.

LAST WORD: SO, IS IT THE SAME AS A BAKER'S DOZEN?

Every so often, I'll get asked, "Isn't a Purple Goldfish just like a baker's dozen? Like when you buy a dozen donuts or bagels and get the thirteenth for free?"

In order to understand the reasoning behind a baker's dozen, we need to travel back to its origin in England. The concept dates back to the thirteenth century during the reign of Henry III. During this time, there was a perceived need for regulations controlling quality, pricing, and checking weights to avoid fraudulent activity. It was common for merchants to cheat customers. The Assize (Statute) of Bread and Ale was instituted to regulate the price, weight, and quality of the bread and beer manufactured and sold in English towns and villages.

Bakers who were found to have shortchanged customers could be liable for severe punishment. The worst of which was having your hand chopped off with an ax.

Photo Credit: **Shutterstock**

To guard against the punishment, the baker would give 13 for the price of 12 to be certain of not being known as a cheat.

The irony is that the statute deals with weight and not quantity. The merchants created the "baker's dozen" to change perception. They understood that one of the 13 could be lost, eaten, burnt, or ruined in some way while still leaving the customer with an actual dozen. The baker wasn't doing it to honor the relationship initially. It was an act of self-preservation to protect their hands.

The problem with a baker's dozen is that it has become expected. Nowadays when you walk into a bakery and buy a dozen bagels, you expect the thirteenth on the house. Therefore, it is not a true Purple Goldfish. Now if you received a 14th bagel as part of the dozen, that would be a Purple Goldfish.

A REVELATION

In looking through over 1,000 examples of customer lagniappe, I made a key realization. It led me to another quest involving employees.

CHAPTER 5

WHY GREEN?

*"I came to see in my time at IBM
that 'culture' isn't just one aspect of the game —
it is the game."*

— Lou Gerstner

Green became the second color in the Goldfish Series in 2013.

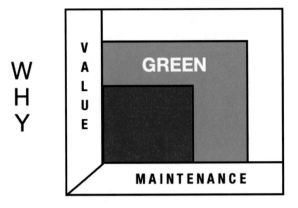

HOW

Green was based on an insight gained during the Purple Goldfish Project. When studying hundreds of brands that did the little extras for customers, it turned out that the best brands did the same thing for employees. In fact, most of those brands put the employees first based on a simple realization. The simple fact is that you can't have happy, enthused customers without happy, engaged employees.

WHY GREEN FOR EMPLOYEES?

Like purple, green is also an official color of Mardi Gras. The selection of colors originates from when the Grand Duke Alexis Romanoff of Russia visited New Orleans in 1872. The Grand Duke came to the city in pursuit of love. He was enamored with an actress named Lydia Thompson.

Born Eliza Hodges Thompson, Lydia was a leading performer on the London stage, and she introduced English burlesques to American audiences in 1868 with her troupe known as the

British Blondes. *The New York Times* called Lydia "a blonde of the purest type, saucy, blue-eyed, golden-haired and of elegant figure."

During his stay in the Crescent City, the Grand Duke was given the honor of selecting the official Mardi Gras colors by the Krewe of Rex. His selection of purple, green, and gold would also later become the colors of the House of Romanoff in Russia. The 1892 Rex Parade theme first gave meaning to the official Mardi Gras colors. Purple was symbolic of justice, gold was symbolic of power, and green was symbolic of faith.

Photo Credit: **Pixabay**

A NEW SEARCH

Not learning my lesson from Purple, I began the search for another 1,001 examples. This time I wanted to crowdsource examples of employee lagniappe. Green Goldfish represented little extras that were designed to drive engagement and reinforce culture beyond compensation.

I didn't have to go far for a world-class example. A few miles across town from my new home of Cary, North Carolina was the largest privately held software company in the world.

The story of that company begins with a young college graduate named James. James received a job working for NASA on the Apollo space program in the late 1960s. Beat the Russians and put a man on the moon, it must have seemed like a dream job.

Until it wasn't...

What James found was a toxic work environment. People didn't communicate and any semblance of trust was absent.

Employees had to use time cards and there were metal detectors to make sure employees weren't stealing. It was even worse when he saw how the executives were treated. They enjoyed special parking areas, break rooms, and their own cafeteria.

James must've felt like a minion.

He watched executives enjoy good "free" coffee, while he and his coworkers had to dump a quarter into a vending machine for brown swill.

The experience would leave a mark. Discouraged, James would head back to North Carolina State University and begin his doctoral studies in statistics. Upon graduating he'd take a position on the faculty. Jame took part in a USDA research project to create a general-purpose statistical analysis system for analyzing agricultural data.

By 1976, the statistical analysis system (SAS) software had 100 clients. He and three other faculty would spin it out and create a company. James would take the role of CEO.

From the outset, James wanted to make his company a fun place to work with the work itself is the biggest reward. Creating an environment that would harness creativity and provide the employees with all of the resources they would need.

From its earliest days, employees tell stories of piling into Dr. Goodnight's station wagon and going down the street for pizza.

SAS would pick up the tab whenever they added another 100 customer sites.

Remembering the culture at NASA, his focus became treating people the way he'd like to be treated. Goodnight believed that if you treat people like they matter... they will.

As we deal with "The Great Resignation," perhaps we can learn from James. He knew that annual turnover could be as high as 30 percent in his industry. And that filling empty positions could cost anywhere from 2x to 5x an employee's salary. At SAS, turnover was typically between 2 to 4 percent.

It was simple math according to Dr. Goodnight, "You have two choices. You can spend money on employees or headhunters and training, and it's about the same amount of money. So why not spend it on the employees?"

It takes more than just a paycheck to keep their people happy.

Dr. James Goodnight believes that money should not be the key motivator for team members. Because people who care primarily about money can easily be bought.

SAS has been recognized annually as one of *Fortune's* Great Places to Work since the inception of the list in 1998. In 2020, Goodnight was awarded a CEO Great Place to Work For All Leadership Award.

His entire approach can be summed up by a SAS employee in *Fast Company*, "You're given the freedom, the flexibility, and the resources to do your job. Because you're treated well, you treat the company well."

All of the benefits and perks are available to all employees, and everyone on campus is a SAS employee: software engineers, salespeople, childcare workers, groundskeepers, and so on.

Founder Goodnight believes strongly that people are much more committed if they are part of the company. All employees have the same exact bonus plan potential.

Here are some examples of the little extras at SAS:

- Free fresh fruit every Monday, M&Ms on Wednesday, and breakfast goodies every Friday. Break rooms are stocked with complimentary soft drinks, juices, crackers, coffee, and tea.

- Employee events and celebrations, including the annual Family Picnic, the elegant Winter Party, and end-of-the-month parties.

- Coffee with Goodnight. Once a month, employees can sign up to sit down with Dr. Goodnight for coffee and biscuits. Eight to 10 employees get randomly selected for the hour-long session.

- SAS cafeteria meals are relatively cheap, and an emphasis is put on healthy food for employees.

THE TWO MOST IMPORTANT FEET IN BUSINESS

Green was based on the importance of having an engaged workforce. After all, where is the value created in business? It's created in the last two feet of a transaction—the space between the employee and the customer.

In 2005, HCL Technologies of India needed a transformational change. New CEO Vineet Nayar decided to make a statement. He set out a new strategy that focused on putting "Employees First."

Vineet understood the importance of interactions between frontline employees and the customer. He referred to this critical distance as the "value zone." The priority at HCL became: Employees first, customers second, management third and shareholders last. His employees on the front line were the key to the HCL turnaround. They were the true custodians of the brand and drivers of customer loyalty. Nayar wanted to shift the focus from the "WHAT" of what HCL offered to the "HOW" of delivering value.

Nayar decided to turn conventional management upside down. They inverted the pyramid and placed employees first at the top. This wasn't just lip service. Vineet engaged in a number of little changes that reinforced the new direction.

These "little things" would be tangible changes on the journey. They are beacons along the voyage that help drive employee engagement and reinforce culture. Nayar drew his inspiration from Mahatma Gandhi and his famous Dandi March. Mahatma walked to the sea to make salt as a protest to the British government about their monopoly on salt production in India. This small action ignited change, becoming a catalyst that led to a large-scale uprising. Nayar knew he needed actions and not words.

OPENING THE WINDOW OF INFORMATION

One of the initiatives that HCL put together was an online forum for employees called U&I. Employees could ask any question to the senior team at HCL. It was an open site where everyone could see the question, the questioner, and the answer. Employees responded favorably, "This is the biggest change we have seen at HCL in years. Now we have a management team that is willing to acknowledge the dirt."

Why open the window of information and show the dirt? Vineet uses the metaphor of an Amsterdam Window. Having previously lived on the Herengracht ("Gentleman's Canal") in Amsterdam, I can attest that these windows are immense. They are a throwback to the modest Calvinist period when subtle expressions of wealth, such as being able to afford to pay the highest window tax, were favored by the rich. In the words of writer Joanna Tweedy, "Today, the centuries-old glass, beautifully imperfect, frames the olive-green waters outside and lets the natural light and the eyes of curious tourists pour in."

Photo Credit: **Pixabay**

On a visit to Amsterdam, Vineet pointed out the windows and asked his friend who lived on the canal, "Why are there no curtains on the large windows?"

His friend mentioned all the obvious reasons like letting in light and enjoying the view of the canal. But then he offered a much more interesting answer, "It keeps the house clean."

It turns out that the bigger your windows, the more glass you have, the more visible your dirt will be—to you and to everyone who visits or passes by. In Vineet's words, "If you can see the dirt, you will be much more likely to get rid of it. A transparent house has a dramatic effect on the culture inside."

Culture trumps strategy and principles beat rules. The entire premise of green in the *Green Goldfish* is that employees must come first. Employee experience should be a priority for leadership.

RECONNECTING WITH TOM

While writing *Purple Goldfish* in 2010, I crossed paths with a friend from college. Tom and I both lived on the second floor of Sheahan Hall during our freshman year at Marist College. Tom brandished a personality and a warm smile that lit up the room. By our Senior Year, he was captaining the football team.

Tom was now a successful businessman, owning an award-winning PR agency. Coyne Public Relations was based in New Jersey and New York City. The agency boasts an impressive list of clients. Tom and his team have worked with iconic brands such as Disney, Campbell Soup, and Burger King.

While sitting down with Tom, I asked him about his business philosophy. Tom relayed an approach that was both simple and prophetic. In Tom's words,

> When I started the agency, my goal was not to be the biggest or to have the best clients. It was simply to become the best agency to work for. I knew if we were the best agency to work for, we would then attract the best people. And that if we retained the best people, the best clients would follow.

The takeaway from Tom was simple. Focus on what you can control—creating a great work environment. That environment or culture will then attract the best people.

SHIFTING YOUR MINDSET

Employees are the bedrock of any organization. You would be better served taking compensation out of the equation and thinking of them as volunteers. Here is a great analysis from Ted Coiné on this exact approach:

CEOs, team leaders, and everyone in-between: if your people don't love your company after four years of employment (or four months, or four quarters), that's all on you .... Do you have the pick of the employment litter? Are your best people dying to stay on board? If not, it isn't that they're ungrateful, and it isn't that your competitors are luring them away. It's that you suck as a leader... Act as if every single employee is a volunteer. Because you know what? In a fundamental way, they are.

15 TYPES OF GREEN GOLDFISH

Similar to Purple, The Green Goldfish Project examined how companies go above and beyond to create signature extras. After collecting over 1,000 examples of employee lagniappe, a few key themes emerged. Specifically, the 15 different types of Green Goldfish can be categorized as the Three B's:

1. Building: Creating a stable environment where people can thrive. Think of these as the foundational building blocks of culture.

2. Belonging: Enabling high-functioning teams and recognizing their efforts. Reinforcing an environment where employees feel like they belong.

3. Becoming: Empowering employees to learn, give back, and take control of their destiny.

Let's have a look at examples of each:

BUILDING: **RECRUITING & ONBOARDING**
Attitudes begin to form at the initial point of contact with an organization. There is no better place to start than when you are recruiting and eventually welcoming new employees to your company. Smart companies take advantage of these early days in order

to ensure a strong, productive, and dedicated workforce. Research shows that employees make the critical decision to stay or leave within the first six months. When new hires participate in an onboarding program, the company can maximize retention, engagement, and productivity.

Example: USAA runs a Boot Camp. The insurance provider for military members and their families has an interesting onboarding process for new employees. Training includes trying on military fatigues, eating MREs (ready-to-eat meals), and reading letters from family members.

BUILDING: **SHELTER**
Pure and simple—space matters. It sets the stage for how you both work and interact on the job. Beyond functionality, the physical environment should be able to tell the story of the company.

Example: TD Bank has the *FlexWorkPlace* program to accommodate changing and flexible work patterns. It features redesigned floors that include more meeting rooms, no traditional offices, and a "collaborative" cafe.

BUILDING: **WELLNESS**
Getting to the heart of your employees involves wellness, little extras designed to support healthy behavior in the workplace and improve health outcomes. Without health, we have nothing.

Example: The Max Borges Agency offers employee benefits such as an onsite gym, fitness classes, and reimbursement for athletic competition entry fees. Founder Max Borges shares, "When you feel good physically... you feel good mentally."

BUILDING: **FOOD & BEVERAGE**
Little things can make a big difference. Even silly little things like M&M's. Food and beverage are a small way to improve engagement.

Example: Team members at Realflow make daily smoothies. The ritual every so often turns into a fun competition where taste and nutrition are the criteria used to judge the winner.

BUILDING: **TIME AWAY**
A recent survey polled over 200 employees from 98 companies to find out what rewards they valued the most. Across all ages and cultures, time off was absolutely number one.

Example: If unlimited vacation is not incentive enough, after five years of working for Red Frog Events, employees are rewarded for their loyalty with a four-week, full-paid trip to Africa, Asia, Europe, or South America for them and a friend.

BUILDING: **MODERN FAMILY**
Families have changed. Today's employers need to prepare for things such as same-sex marriage, infertility, adoption, parental leave, daycare, and eldercare. Making certain that employees can focus on their families reduces stress and keeps workers on a more even keel. This allows them to feel supported and focused on the tasks at hand.

Example: Stew Leonard's offers "Mom's Hours," enabling mothers to work while their children are in school and take off the whole summer to be with them.

BUILDING: **TRANSPARENCY**
Of seventy-five possible drivers of employee engagement, the ONE that was rated as the most important was the extent to which employees believed that their senior management had a sincere interest in their well-being. Transparency is key to engaging employees and winning trust.

Example: Rand Corporation offers an open-door policy at all levels of the organization. Anyone can make an appointment to meet with the CEO, Executive VP, or any of the other VP staff. The company leadership hosts small group lunch meetings as well as coffee get-togethers for open Q&A.

BELONGING: **FLEXIBILITY**
Flexibility is about control, and everyone wants flex. According to research, if there's one work perk that rises above the rest, it's flexible work arrangements.

Example: The furniture retailer IKEA offers a range of alternative work options to help employees balance work-life commitments, including flexible hours, compressed workweek options, and job-sharing arrangements.

BELONGING: **TEAM BUILDING**
Success is frequently seen as a purely individual achievement, often at the expense of others. But in the corporate world, an organization can only thrive with the collective help of everyone. For employees, being part of a team helps create a sense of belonging.

Example: At Virginia company Snagajob, the Culture Squad organizes the annual Office Olympics, during which employees [Snaggers] are divided into competing nations—and dress the part.

BELONGING: **ATTABOYS AND ATTAGIRLS**
Reaching the heart of your employees involves recognition. "YOU MATTER." These two words can change your mood, change your mind, and have the power to change lives if we leverage them in the right way.

Example: Fishbowl Fridays are held each week at LaBreche. Employees give kudos to each other for simple, everyday things that are done extraordinarily or out-of-the-park big hits.

BECOMING: **TRAINING AND DEVELOPMENT**
Investing in your employees involves training and development. Going the extra mile to allow employees to learn how to become the best version of themselves.

Example: The Container Store puts an emphasis on training. Employees receive an average of 160+ hours per year. Typical annual turnover in retail is 100 percent, but at Container Store, it hovers around 15-20 percent.

BECOMING: **PAYING IT FORWARD**
Embracing purpose and giving back to society are strong drivers of employee engagement.

Example: Employees at National Rural Electric Cooperative Association are encouraged to volunteer. For every 24 hours of time an employee gives to charity, he or she receives an extra vacation day.

BECOMING: **EMPOWERING DREAMS AND GOALS**
Help people find direction, support them, and then get out of their way. In one word—EMPOWERMENT.

Example: Zappos provides a life coach for employees.

EMPLOYEE LAGNIAPPE

Motivation for employees is sagging. Recent reports show that motivation has fallen off at more than half of all companies. In difficult economic times, how can companies boost employee morale and drive high performance? The simple answer is doing the little extras beyond compensation to demonstrate commitment to your employees.

Here is a great quote by Vince Burks of Amica Insurance explaining this exact focus:

> The concept of lagniappe is not just a part of our brand ethos; it is ingrained in everything we do. It, therefore, extends to our most valued resource—our employees. In fact, that is the secret to our success. Excellent benefits. Advancement opportunities. A real work/life

balance. And an open and regular line of communication with each other and with senior management. Taken together, we give our employees all that they need to succeed...and more. This is absolutely essential. Satisfied employees lead to satisfied customers. Long-term employees lead to long-term relationships with customers. And pride, trust, and morale are all contagious. Further, well-trained, long-term employees know how to get the job done quickly, efficiently, and effectively. They know their customers. They know their colleagues. They know their company. And they, therefore, know how to 'get to yes' with ease and a sense of grace. This is good for the customer. This is good for the company.

Satisfied employees do indeed lead to satisfied customers. Green Goldfish are "little extras" for staff that help build a dynamic, healthy culture.

ANOTHER REVELATION

I used to think that you should treat all of your customers and all of your employees the same. I no longer believe that's the best approach. This revelation led me to the third color in the initial book trilogy.

CHAPTER 6

WHY GOLDEN?

*"The law of the vital few
and the trivial many."*

- Joseph Juran

Gold became the third color in the Series in 2014.

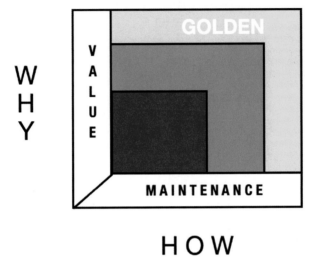

Why gold? Similar to Purple and Green, Gold is an ode to the birth-place of the word lagniappe [New Orleans] and the colors of its most famous event [Mardi Gras]. Gold was symbolic of power.

Golden Goldfish was based on an important insight. I used to think that all employees and all customers were equal. But research shows that for most companies, 80 percent of profitability comes from just 20 percent of customers. And 80 percent of the value generated in an organization typically comes from just 20 percent of employees. Based on this realization, I now think differently. You shouldn't treat everyone the same, we should treat everyone fairly. I learned this approach from an unlikely place... a vegetable garden.

LESSONS FROM A PEA PLANT

The setting is Paris 1848. A boy is born of an exiled noble Geno-ese family. His father, Raffaele was an Italian civil engineer who had fled Italy like other Italian nationalists. His mother, Marie was French. Enthusiastic about the German revolution that year, Raf-faele and Marie named their son Fritz Wilfried.

Fritz would move back to Italy with his family at age 10. He would grow up to become an engineer, sociologist, economist, political scientist, and philosopher. He would change his name to the Italian of Wilfried... Vilfredo. During his life, he would make several important contributions to economics, particularly in the study of income distribution.

His legacy as an economist was profound. Vilfredo's books looked more like modern economics than most other texts of that day. They were filled with tables of statistics, rows of integral signs and equations, and intricate graphs. Partly because of his work, the field of economics evolved from a branch of moral philosophy, as practiced by Adam Smith, into a data-intensive field. Vilfredo is credited with helping to develop the field of microeconomics. He is perhaps the first data scientist.

But just over a century ago Vilfredo would stumble across an idea that would change the course of history. This revelation would come from a simple observation in his vegetable garden. One day while walking through his garden, the 59-year-old Vilfredo noticed something peculiar about his pea plant. This simple observation quickly turned into action as he began to pick all of the pods off the plant. When opening each he made an interesting discovery. Vilfredo found that 80 percent of his peas came from a mere 20 percent of his pods. This intrigued the Italian economist.

Soon he was applying this ratio to other socioeconomic scenarios. You may now recognize his last name. His full name was Vilfredo Federico Damaso Pareto and his most famous finding was that 20 percent of the people in Italy owned 80 percent of the land.

Pareto's discovery and contribution were largely unheralded until two decades after his death. During World War II, social scientist Joseph Moses Juran uncovered his work while streamlining shipment processes for the Lend-Lease Administration in Washington,

D.C. Juran found that 80 percent of the defects in shipments were attributed to just 20 percent of the causes. He began to look for the ration in other places. Juran was the first to coin the phrases, *"Pareto's Law of Unequal Distribution"* and the *"80/20 rule."*

THE VITAL FEW

Juran's most important application came within the field of quality control. He noticed that the majority of defects with the shipments came from a small percentage of the total causes. Juran famously referred to Pareto's Principle as, *"The law of the vital few and the trivial many."*

Gold represents the little things you do for your top 20 percent of employees and customers. Similar to the *Purple Goldfish* and *Green Goldfish*, the *Golden Goldfish* provides the following three benefits:

1. Differentiation – a way to stand out in a sea of sameness. Give the company a REMARK-able difference or set of signature differences.

2. Retention – if you keep employees and customers happy, they'll stick around longer.

3. Word of Mouth – create a culture that attracts talent and referrals.

ALL CUSTOMERS ARE NOT CREATED EQUAL

Eighty percent of your profitability comes from 20 percent of your customers. In the words of Joseph Juran, these customers are your "vital few." Imagine you have five different types of customers represented by geese. Four of those geese are white and one is gold. That Golden Goose represents your most important customers. And it's not even close. They are laying a golden egg for you each and every day. Neglect them or treat them like everyone else at your own peril.

9 TYPES OF GOLDEN GOLDFISH

I smartened up this go-around. Instead of crowdsourcing 1,001 examples, I focused on collecting 200 strong examples in the Golden Goldfish Project. When reviewing them, I discovered there are nine ways to provide signature added value for your vital few.

The first five focus on customers:

#1 **THROW-IN'S**

Throw-ins are the little extras for your best customers. Want a case study that drives this point home? Forgive me, it's a bit cheesy.

In 2012, the processed cheese brand experienced its third consecutive year of declining sales. Whoops. What could Kraft do to reverse this trend?

1. Should they get new or lapsed customers to try the product? Perhaps use sampling and discounts.

2. Should they get infrequent purchasers to buy the product more consistently? Perhaps focus on recipes and coupons.

3. Or should they focus on frequent users who loved the product? Perhaps find ways to get them to buy more Velveeta products.

When the brand managers studied how the brand was being consumed, they were shocked. The research found the top 10 percent of Velveeta buyers account for over 50 percent of all profit for the product. And here was the kicker... these consumers were not getting enough Velveeta in their lives.

Kraft decided to focus on this key segment of 2.4 million consumers. The results were anything but cheesy.

New product spin-offs totaling over $100 million in additional sales in the next 18 months were a game-changer for the brand. It shifted a paradigm for Kraft.

According to Kraft marketing director Greg Gallagher, "The previous thinking was that the quickest, easiest path to growth was to identify light users or lapsed users. But when we talked to superconsumers, we learned that in fact, they wanted to use Velveeta more— they were starving for it."

TAKEAWAY: All customers and employees are not created equal. Do more for your best ones. In the words of Eddie Yoon, Steve Carlotti, and Dennis Moore in *Harvard Business Review*, "Show the love to those that love you the most." These employees and customers are your vital few. They represent your golden goose. You don't treat all of your geese the same, you treat them all fairly.

#2 ADDED SERVICE

Added service is the little extra service included with a transaction.

Example: Virgin Atlantic
Flyte Tyme has a very unique partnership with Virgin Atlantic. If you are a first-class or top tier client of Virgin Atlantic, the airline offers free car service within 75 miles of the airport. In addition, the driver calls Virgin Atlantic 15 minutes out with the number of bags the person has. When they arrive at the curb, they are greeted by the airline. Right there Virgin tags the luggage and checks it in.

#3 FOLLOW UP

Follow up is an expression of thanks. It is a personal gesture conveying appreciation and acknowledgment.

Example: Maker's Mark

Maker's Mark does a little extra to cultivate advocacy with its best customers. The manufacturer has a unique ambassador program. Its best customers can take a pledge to share the love of Maker's Mark with family and friends. Sworn in ambassadors' names are etched on a brass plate and placed on a new barrel. Maker's allows the ambassadors to follow the whole process of creation. After six or seven years, Maker's follows up and the ambassadors are invited to come back and pick up a bottle or two of the aged bourbon from their barrel. Of course, one of the ultimate hands-on perks is picking up your bottle and dipping it into the signature red wax.

#4 CONVENIENCE

Little ways to remove friction and become easier to do business with.

Example: Disney Magic Hours

Every day, one of the Disney World theme parks opens an hour early and/or two hours later. These times are called Disney's extra magic hours. The added golden goldfish is for Disney Resort guests only.

#5 HANDLING MISTAKES

Proactively handling mistakes creates advocates.

Example: Boloco

Boloco is a brand that deploys surprise and delight around the clock. This Boston-based restaurant chain isn't shy about offering freebies to compensate for messing up an order for valued customers. The company keeps an ear out for less-than-completely-satisfied feedback and bends over backward to make things right. Is the salsa mysteriously missing from your burrito? A free menu item will be magically added to your rewards card.

The next four types of Golden Goldfish focus on employees:

#6 FLEXIBILITY

Providing your best employees with the freedom to organize how they work.

Example: Scottrade
Roll with the punches and moves. Countless workers have made a geographical move to get or keep a job, but jobs don't generally move to follow employees. St. Louis-based online investing firm, Scottrade, will consider opening a new branch in an area an employee is moving to. According to *Fortune*, Scottrade has opened over 20 offices for employees. In one instance, a star employee moved twice, to Georgia and Florida, and Scottrade opened offices in both locations.

#7 RECOGNITION

Little ways to recognize the efforts and contributions of your best employees.

Example: Etana
South African insurance company Etana has its own unique annual program called REDwards. The awards honor the efforts of employees who have gone above and beyond by living the values of the brand. The actual awards are made by local artists and are given out to reinforce the core values. The company has featured winners on billboards near their offices.

#8 TRAINING & DEVELOPMENT

Small things to invest in the development of your best employees.

Example: Centro Media

The Chicago-based online advertising buyer focuses on the manager-employee relationship. Centro Media spends a lot of time training managers. Scott Golas, Vice President of Human Resources shares "Let's face it: People leave companies because of their boss. We try to remove the typical obstacles (between bosses and employees) by sharing more information, by providing great training, and by making sure those bosses have the right skill sets."

#9 EMPOWERMENT

Empowerment is about the little ways to engage your top employees.

Example: 3M Science Fair

Once a year, hundreds of employees from dozens of divisions at 3M make cardboard posters. Those posters describe their 15 percent time project as if they were presenting volcano models at a middle school science fair. After they stand up their poster, they hang out next to it, awaiting feedback, suggestions, and potential co-collaborators. Wayne Maurer is an R&D manager in 3M's abrasives division and calls it a chance for people to unhinge their "inner geek." He elaborates, "For technical people, it's the most passionate and engaged event we have at 3M."

Gold is about recognizing your best employees and customers. Doing the little things for those you value the most. That you shouldn't treat everyone the same, but treat everyone fairly within the realm of value and maintenance. Once you've mastered this, you are ready for the middle level of the Black Matrix. Let's turn our attention to warmth and competence next.

CHAPTER 7

WARMTH AND COMPETENCE

*"For the first time in history,
the entire world is wired in a way that is
consistent with the way evolution
has wired us to think and behave."*

- Chris Malone

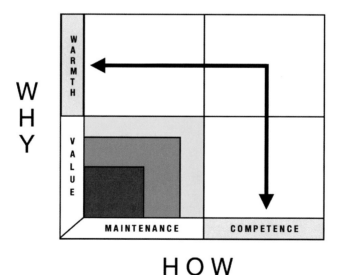

For the overwhelming majority of human history, commerce between humans was conducted face-to-face.

Along the way, humans developed the ability to quickly judge the intentions and abilities of others based on their words, appearance, facial expressions, and body language. The choices that buyers made were as much about the person involved and their relationship with them, as it was the product or service they were offering. For thousands of years to quote *The Mandalorian,* "This is the way."

However, in the mid-19th century, the Industrial Revolution came along and disrupted commerce. Along with the growth and efficiency brought about by mass production, mass distribution, and mass communication, the frequency of face-to-face human contact in business steadily declined with it. In hindsight, it's now clear that industrialization has led to a mass dehumanization of trade between people, yet the basic psychology that guides human choices remains unchanged.

We are still wired to make choices based on the intentions and abilities of others. Yet we are largely starved of the human contact that helps us make those decisions easy and natural. So, despite that we have more information than ever before and more ways to communicate than ever before, both customer and employee loyalty is lower than ever before in just about every industry.

But now after decades of what author Chris Malone calls the "Middle Ages of Marketing," a new Relationship Renaissance has emerged between customers, employees, and companies. Ecommerce, social networks, and mobile devices are bringing us "Back to the Future" to an environment where we have access to much more information and direct contact with the people behind the products and services we do business with.

As a result, we are again making more and more choices based on the people we are dealing with and our relationship with them, rather than the product or service alone. So, after 150 years of fairly rapid industrialization, we are now coming full circle to a place where social accountability and person-to-person connections are again at the forefront of business. The connections are turbocharged by digital communication.

The problem is that commerce hasn't been conducted this way for generations and much of what we've been taught and trained about business isn't working anymore in this "new" but quite ancient social environment. So, our challenge is to learn different ways of conducting business that is better aligned with the natural triggers of human trust and loyalty.

ENTER WARMTH AND COMPETENCE

In our evolution as humans, we were forced to develop skills integral to our survival. One of those skills was the ability to make snap judgments about our surroundings with a high degree of speed and accuracy. As we walked out of the *"cave"* our senses went immediately into survival mode. We judged everyone and everything we encountered on two basic criteria:

1. *Are they a threat?*

2. *What was their ability to carry out that threat?*

This basic truth is at the heart of the book *The Human Brand* by Chris Malone and Susan T. Fiske. Their research, built upon work done by Dr. Bogdan Wojciszke, has shown that over 80 percent of our judgments are based on these two factors. It boils down to our perception of 1. **warmth** and 2. **competence**. These perceptions don't just apply to people. We also apply the same standards to companies and how we perceive our experience with them. We automatically judge their behaviors on a subconscious level.

FROM THE LOCAL VILLAGE TO THE MASS MARKET TO A GLOBAL VILLAGE

The mass market is a relatively new phenomenon. Merely 150 years ago we consumed almost everything made from people we know. The reputation of a merchant was as precious as gold. If a small business wronged you, everyone in the local village would quickly know about it. Merchants faced public censure, potential ruin, and even losing a limb. As a result, businesses worked hard to establish trust and earn repeat business.

But then the mass market emerged. Almost everything we consumed was made by a faceless, far-off company. There was no voice of the customer. We were powerless to expose or punish brands that acted badly. Outside of lodging a complaint with the Better Business Bureau or writing consumer advocates like Ralph Nader, we were handcuffed.

Enter Digital, Social, and Mobile. The Internet has changed the game. In the words of Chris Malone, "For the first time in history, the entire world is wired in a way that is consistent with the way evolution has wired us to think and behave." Social media has flattened the earth. Each consumer has the opportunity to share his or her experiences with millions of others. It has caused a huge ripple effect in our global village.

Brands today must find ways to get beyond the basics of just adding value and reducing maintenance. The next step is to level up to demonstrate warmth and reinforce competence.

Let's look at how technology can play a role with competence.

CHAPTER 8

WHY BLUE?

"Big data gives you trends to make major decisions.
Little data gives you information to keep your best customers coming back.
It's that simple. The question is really about whether or not a company is
willing to invest in technology and analysis to recognize customer preferences
and are then willing to train employees to deliver an experience based on this
information."

- Shep Hyken CSP, CPAE

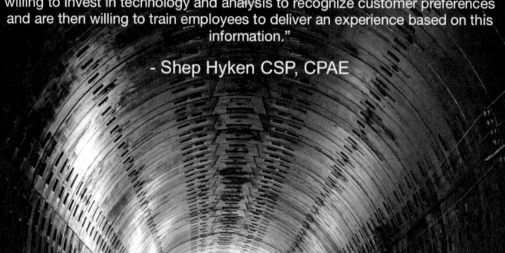

Blue was the fourth color in the Goldfish Series in 2016. It was inspired by my time working with IBM as part of their Futurist program. I began to see the role that technology and data were beginning to play in improving the customer experience.

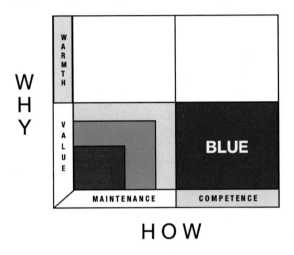

Why blue? To fully explain the reasoning behind blue we must rewind all the way back to the 10th century.

King Harald Gormsson ruled Denmark in the 10th century. The medieval king was notorious for uniting all of Scandinavia and converting the Danes to Christianity. Legend has it that King Harald had a nasty dead tooth that turned blue over time. This earned him the nickname Blåtand. Blåtand is Danish for Blue Tooth.

Fast-forward a Millenium to 1996. A consortium of companies including Intel, Ericsson, IBM, and Nokia came together to create a new short-range wireless industry standard. They wanted to avert the disaster that was Beta versus VHS in the world of video. The group faced a challenge to name the new common standard.

In 1997, the first step towards solving the problem came about in Toronto at a conference. Two of the engineers working on the project ended up going out for a night on the town. Intel's Jim

Kardach met up with Ericsson engineer Sven Mattisson. Kardach had been working on a program called Business-RF and Mattisson had developed a comparable standard called MC Links. Over the course of the evening, the discussion turned to history. Mattisson had just read a book called The Longships by Frans G. Bengtsson. The book chronicled the travels of warriors serving King Harald. Upon learning about the interesting nickname, Kardach perked up, "It occurred to me that this would make a good codename for the program." Mattison agreed and soon Kardach was pitching the idea to others in the group. After much debate and no consensus, the group decided that Bluetooth would be the placeholder.

Later they would agree to use IBM's idea of "PAN." PAN was an acronym for Personal Area Networking. But it turned out that PAN presented both intellectual property and SEO challenges. Again, Bluetooth became the working name until marketing decided on a different name. It never happened. Bluetooth became the standard-bearer that we recognize today.

King Harald would have been proud that his 10th-century nickname would become a 21st century fixture. His mark also appears on the Bluetooth logo, which is the Nordic letters H and B combined together into a bindrune. Drop the mark on a blue background and you have the familiar Bluetooth logo seen on millions of devices around the world.

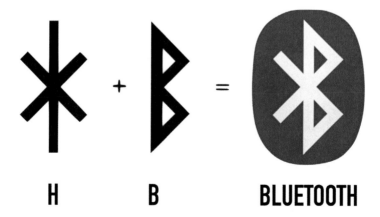

H   B   BLUETOOTH

All because of a good king and his bad tooth.

The color blue highlights convergence, just as Bluetooth was the result of a consortium and how King Harald united Scandinavia. In our case, convergence represents technology. How big data and little data can deliver notable trends and personalized insights to improve the customer experience.

KNOWLEDGE AND AGILITY

Customer experience has become the new battleground for competitive advantage in business. But with every wise company focusing on customer experience, how do you stand out and differentiate? You need to find ways to demonstrate competence.

Former GE CEO, the late Jack Welch perhaps said it best, "There are only two sources of competitive advantage: the ability to learn more about our customers faster than the competition and the ability to turn that learning into action faster than the competition." Competitive advantage then must come from knowledge and agility in business.

INFO-SENSE AND NBO'S

Info-sense is "the ability to utilize data to really understand customers as people and personalize their service." Coined by Trend-Watching.com, this sixth-sense capability enables companies to learn more about customers' individual needs into action in real-time. Companies who embrace info-sense can provide customers with exactly what they need right when they need it.

The shift to info-sense should be good news for businesses. The benefit is simple. It typically costs one-tenth of the amount of money to upsell a current customer you know than it does to acquire a new one.

Want an example of a brand driving business through info-sense? Enter Westpac.

An Australian financial services provider, Westpac is one of Australia's big four and the second-largest bank in New Zealand. With over 14 million customers, they have well over 100 million customer interactions per month. The bank has been able to connect the dots and embrace info-sense. They leveraged their immense amount of customer data with a program called "Know Me."

The bank understands what a customer needs at different life stages and moments of truth in their customer journey. The bank uses technology, data, and analytics to drive insights about its customers.

These insights allow them to create NBO's (next best offers). By using a mix of offline transactional data and online behavioral data, the insights allow the bank to predict what the customer might need next. Standing NBOs appear in Westpac's front-line systems. When a customer interacts with a bank teller or customer service representative, the employee extends the offer.

Despite high confidence in these personalized offers, Westpac knows a 100 percent close rate is unreasonable. They also understand that a one percent conversion creates a poor customer experience. In the first year of "Know Me," Westpac converted 46 percent of offers. There's no doubt that using big data trends and little data insights helped identify a range of personalized "next best offers" and ultimately delivered millions to Westpac's bottom line.

Westpac practices what many companies do not. They use a combination of big data and little data to provide a better experience for their customers. Blue is about helping you do the same for your organization.

RISING CUSTOMER EXPECTATIONS

Customer expectations are binary. You either exceed them, or you fall short. Similarly, if you're just trying to keep up with increasing consumer expectations, you're fighting an uphill battle.

Amazon knows this. Their objective isn't to meet the expectation of competence. Rather, their objective is to exceed customer expectations such that customer expectations increase by way of the service they provide. Scot Wingo, Co-Founder of ChannelAdvisor, calls this increasing level of customer expectation the "Amazon Effect."

THE EMPOWERED ON-DEMAND CUSTOMER

Fueled largely by the Amazon Effect, the expectations of today's customers are rising at a dramatic pace. They expect a personalized, quick, and consistent experience. An IBM Institute for Business Value report brings this fact into sharp focus. The report found the following:

- 76 percent of consumers expect organizations to understand their individual needs

- 81 percent of consumers demand improved response time

- 68 percent anticipate organizations will harmonize consumer experiences

Empowered customers are starting to take for granted that a company will know and understand their individual needs. They expect that companies will know what they searched for and their past ordering history. Amazon has raised the bar on customer expectations.

David Trice refers to this new breed of need-it-now consumers as On-Demand customers. Today's customer expects companies will address their needs with precision and expertise at every touchpoint. Companies that leverage info-sense can expect increased customer loyalty and advocacy. The penalty for non-performers is more than just a lost customer as social media now provides a platform for any unhappy consumer to broadcast their bad experience globally.

To offset the Amazon Effect, you must get ahead of the expectations curve. You don't have to deliver Amazon-level service, but you must know that expectations are increasing, and you have to stay one step ahead.

TODAY'S CONSUMER

When thinking about all of the innovations from the last 50 years, two facts come into sharp focus. First, the rate of innovation is ever increasing. What would seem like a giant leap fifty years ago appears more like a small step today. Second, these innovations are changing the average consumer. Going from a world where connected technology was mostly a dream to such ubiquity where more humans have mobile phones than access to working toilets is nothing short of impressive.

As you consider the customer journey, there's no doubt that consumer expectations have changed—we've forced them to change with each innovation being faster, smaller, and more accessible than the last. The same expectations apply to your business.

Customers now expect faster response times, shorter wait times, more value, and less cost all at once. The companies who figure out how to serve this modern consumer will thrive. And the others? Their days are numbered.

Blue Goldfish highlights those companies doing the former, using technology, data, and analytics to demonstrate competence and improve the customer experience. Technology brought us these increasing expectations. It may be the only thing that can save us.

THE THREE R'S

The Blue Goldfish Project revealed 300 examples of how companies leverage technology, data, and analytics to improve the customer experience. It became clear that the eight different ways could be grouped into three main categories. The three R's of:

1. Relationship

2. Responsiveness

3. Readiness

Here are descriptions and an example of each type:

RELATIONSHIP

1. **Personalization:** combining big data and little data to provide customers with products or services that meet their individual needs.

   Example: understanding a customer's budget, taste, and lifestyle to deliver a monthly selection of unique clothes and accessories from Stitch Fix.

2. **Personal Data/Behavior Change:** using customers' personal data to provide them with an opportunity for transformative change.

   Example: track your healthy activities and turn them into lower life insurance premiums at John Hancock.

RESPONSIVENESS

1. **Customer Service 3.0:** leveraging technology, data, and analytics to proactively deliver the next level of customer service.

   Example: Delta Air Lines has a mobile app that proactively delivers flight notifications and allows customers to rebook without having to call or wait in line at the airport. All of these proactive communications can reduce high call or email volumes as well as social media complaints.

2. **Waiting:** using technology to shorten wait times or help them pass more quickly.

   Example: order your coffee in advance using the Starbucks app and they'll have your coffee waiting for you when you arrive.

3. **Real-time Response:** monitoring and responding to real-time data to tackle (and maybe even prevent) hurdles for your customers.

   Example: helping prevent delinquency on loan payments by monitoring a daily report that tracks Pioneer Federal Credit Union's customers' loans. PFCU uses the report data to predict delinquency and be proactive in helping customers meet their commitments before it happens

READINESS

1. **Frictionless Commerce:** making it as smooth and easy as possible to do business with you.

   Example: minimizing the sad faces of disappointment when your favorite flavor of Izzy's Ice Cream isn't available by implementing an RFID system that updates menu boards and automatically notifies customers who've requested to opt-in.

2. **Location-Aware Convenience:** collecting location information from customers to provide them with a customized experience.

   Example: Tesla cars calculate how far you can drive based on your current charge, your current location, and your proximity to a charging station.

3. **Trust and Safety:** using technology to keep customers safe.

   Example: the confirmation email that Safelite sends includes the technician's name, bio, credentials, and a photograph. You can also track the technician like an Uber or Lyft.

BIG DOORS SWING ON LITTLE HINGES

Technology, data, and analytics can be game-changers. The more you know, the faster you can respond. And the ability to anticipate allows you to create meaningful differentiation for the customer you serve. So can leveraging purpose to reinforce warmth. Let's look at how.

CHAPTER 9

WHY RED?

"Well run, values-centered businesses can contribute to humankind in more tangible ways than any other organization in society."

- Bill George

Red became the fifth color in the Goldfish Series in 2017. If *Blue Goldfish* focused on competence, *Red Goldfish* is about warmth and understanding your "Why" in business.

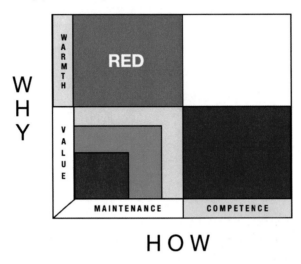

Why red? Red is the color of blood. It's been historically associated with sacrifice and courage. In the US and Europe, red also represents passion, whereas, in Asia, it symbolizes happiness and good fortune. We have to go farther afield for our source. The inspiration for red comes from Africa.

(RED) was created by Bono and Bobby Shriver. Launched at the World Economic Forum in 2006, its purpose was to engage the private sector and its marketing prowess in order to raise funds for the fight against AIDS in Africa. On the back of a napkin, they outlined their idea for a unique union of brands and consumers.

The plan had three goals:

- Provide consumers with a choice that made giving effortless
- Generate profits and a sense of purpose for partner companies
- Create a source of sustainable income for the Global Fund to fund the fight against AIDS

The branding agency Wolff Olins helped build the platform for (RED). They created a unique brand architecture that united participating businesses by literally multiplying their logos to the power (RED). Global brands such as Apple, Nike, Dell, American Express, and The Gap came on board. The appeal of (RED) was clear: it allowed them to tap into a purpose beyond their own profit.

In the words of Wolff Olins, "The appeal of (RED) was clear: it connected these corporations with a purpose beyond their own profit. Some partners went as far as manufacturing products or packaging in African countries, generating jobs, and opportunities for local people."

Red represents the simple idea that brands can be a force for good in the world. They can have a greater purpose beyond striving for profit to always be in the black.

TALE OF ED

It was the spring of 2013 and my first year as an author and speaker. I was introduced to S. Chris Edmonds by a mutual friend. I mentioned to Chris that I was working on launching my business as a keynote speaker and workshop facilitator. He recommended that I speak to Mark Levy.

Mark Levy leads a consulting practice called Levy Innovation focused on positioning. Levy has worked with prominent thought leaders such as Marshall Goldsmith, Simon Sinek, and Cali Yost. I hired Mark to help me develop my speaking and training platform.

Mark is brilliant. He taught me a great deal about understanding my big idea. We spent a considerable amount of time on not only the what and how, but also the why. To illustrate the importance, Mark shared a story about one of his clients. It was one I'd never forget.

THE POWER OF PURPOSE

The client was a financial planner for small business owners. Let's call him Ed. Ed had shared with Mark that he recruited the majority of his new clients by speaking. He would give a 90-minute seminar on managing finances. At the end of the seminar, Ed would offer a free one-hour consultation. If there were 40 people in the room, he'd typically have only two or three take him up on the offer. The need to grow his client base led him to Mark.

As they began to work together, Mark asked Ed why he chose to pursue a career in accounting. Ed shared that his parents had passed away in a car accident and he was raised by his grandparents. His grandfather had worked at a local company for over 30 years. His grandmother was working as an office administrative assistant in a local school. Ed could remember sitting in his living room at age 14 like it was yesterday.

His grandfather was next to him reading the newspaper. An advertisement caught his eye. The ad was for the sale of a local butcher shop. He approached his wife and expressed his desire to purchase the business. They both would quit their jobs and go into business for themselves. She was skeptical but eventually agreed.

Ed watched his grandparents cash in their life savings to start the new business. The butcher shop didn't make any money the first year, lost money in year two, and a little more in year three. By the end of the fifth year, they had lost their remaining capital and were forced to declare bankruptcy. Instead of enjoying their retirement, his grandparents went back to full-time jobs and both worked until they passed away. Ed shared that he went into accounting because he didn't want to have other small business owners experience what had happened to his grandparents. Mark asked Ed to share this personal backstory during his next seminar. The results were staggering. Ed merely told his backstory on why he became a financial planner before starting his regular session. At the end, he made his usual pitch. The difference was that 37 out of the 40 attendees took him up on the offer, many of whom became clients for Ed.

Those attendees understood the "Why" behind Ed's work.

THE SEARCH FOR PURPOSE

Why are we here? This is perhaps the greatest question of all. It has been pondered since the earliest days of human existence. It is our search for meaning in this world. Each one of us is challenged to answer this question. Mark Twain once said that the two most important days in our lives are the day we are born…and the day we find out why. Should the "why" question apply to business? I believe that answer is a resounding YES.

Why are companies in business? What or who comes first in business? Where should you focus? I believe we are on the cusp of the 4.0 version of business. How did we get to this point? Let's explore the progression.

The first school of thought is the 1.0 version.

The 1.0 version in the evolution of business was a shareholder-first mindset. The sole purpose of a company was to maximize profits. The late economist Milton Friedman became its foremost proponent. He famously shared in his *New York Times* article in 1970 that, "there is one and only one social responsibility of business to use its resources and engage in activities designed to increase its profits so long as it stays within the rules of the game, which is to say, engages in open and free competition without deception or fraud." Profit was the prized goal of business. Friedman excoriated leaders who sought anything beyond profits as "unwitting puppets of the intellectual forces that have been undermining the basis of a free society." Business leaders who pursued social interests were guilty of spending money that wasn't their own. Friedman branded them as "unelected government officials" who were illegally taxing employers and customers. The simple goal of business was to provide a return to shareholders. Friedman believed that doing good was incompatible with doing well for your shareholders.

The 2.0 version of business sees profit as an end result, not the goal.

The next evolution of business puts the focus squarely on customers first. Companies should be dedicated to the business of getting and keeping customers. This focus places importance on the overall customer experience and managing ongoing relationships. In the words of Walmart's founder, Sam Walton, "There is only one boss. The customer. And he can fire everybody in the company from the chairman on down, simply by spending his money somewhere else."

Want an example of a company that puts its customers first? Look no further than Amazon. It's the focus of their mission: "We seek to be Earth's most customer-centric company." Founder Jeff Bezos puts customers first and profits second. "We're not competitor obsessed, we're customer-obsessed. We start with the customer and we work backward...We've had three big ideas at Amazon that we've stuck with for years, and they're the reason we're successful: Put the customer first. Invent. And be patient." says Bezos.

This obsession with customers dates back to the earliest days at Amazon. There is always an empty chair in company meetings. The chair at the table represents the customer. The message is clear; the current customer is always top of mind and seen as the most important person in the room.

Peter Drucker made a similar argument for a customer-first focus in his classic book, *Management,* when he wrote, "There is only one valid definition of business purpose: to create a customer... It is the customer who determines what a business is. It is the customer alone whose willingness to pay for a good or for a service converts economic resources into wealth, things into goods...The customer is the foundation of a business and keeps it in existence."

The 3.0 version of business places employees first.

The next version of business puts employees and culture at the forefront. It's rooted in understanding where value is created in an organization. It's created in the last two feet of a transaction, the space between the employee and the customer.

A focus on employees first is based on the idea that culture trumps strategy in an organization. The experience of your employees becomes paramount as it dictates your overall culture. In today's workplace, up to 70 percent of workers are either not engaged or are actively disengaged. To be successful, you need employees who are engaged to create a strong customer experience. According to Ted Coiné, author of *Five Star Customer Service*, "You can't create happy enthused customers without happy engaged employees."

The next evolution of business places purpose as the critical first piece of the puzzle.

The 4.0 version of business places purpose first.

Companies that have a strong, defined purpose find that it drives employee engagement, connects with customers, and fuels the bottom line. According to Deloitte Global CEO Punit Renjen, "Exceptional firms have always been good at aligning their purpose with their execution, and as a result, have enjoyed category leadership in sales and profits." John Kotter and James Heskett demonstrated in their book *Corporate Culture & Performance*, that purposeful, value-driven companies outperform their counterparts in stock price by a factor of 12.

Purpose relates to your "Why" as a business. To quote Simon Sinek, "People don't buy what you do or how you do it, they buy why you do it." It should permeate everything you do. "Every decision should be looked at in terms of purpose. Some decisions may be purpose neutral. But purpose is certainly not just a marketing issue or positioning of your brand image. Purpose should impact every aspect of the firm," says Raj Sisodia, author of *Conscious Capitalism.*

Embracing purpose can become a driver of employee engagement. Daniel Pink touched on the importance of purpose in his book *Drive.* Pink said there are three things that motivate people: autonomy, mastery, and purpose. He believes that purpose is perhaps the greatest of the three because a strong purpose allows you to overcome obstacles and persevere towards a goal.

A NEW WAY FORWARD

The old view of business was a profit-first mindset. You put shareholders first, customers second, employees third, and purpose fourth in terms of focus.

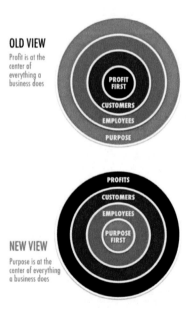

OLD VIEW
Profit is at the center of everything a business does

The new view of business going forward calls for a purpose-first mindset. You put purpose at the center of everything the business does. Then, employees come second and customers third. Taking care of those three, sustainable profit becomes the result as opposed to the sole aim.

NEW VIEW
Purpose is at the center of everything a business does

Purpose is more than a trend or passing fad. Purpose is emerging as a guiding light that can help businesses navigate and thrive in the 21st century. According to the EY Beacon Institute Pursuit of Purpose Study, "Purpose — an aspirational reason for being that is grounded in humanity — is at the core of how many companies are responding to the business and societal challenges of today."

Companies that have a defined purpose benefit from a win-win-win scenario. By standing for something bigger than their products/services, they are winning on three levels:

Win #1: Employees - Purpose helps attract the best talent, keeps them engaged, and retains them. It is important to employees. It helps determine the values of an organization. According to PwC: 6 out of 7 employees would consider leaving an employer whose values no longer met their expectations.

Win #2: Customers – Purpose becomes a differentiator that drives acquisition and retention. It also helps the business stay competitive. It provides a reason for their customers to engage with the business. Purpose is important to customers as it showcases the values of an organization.

According to Brand Fuel: All things being equal, 6 out of 7 customers will choose to do business with companies whose values mesh with their own.

Win #3: Shareholders - Purpose has positive effects on key performance drivers. Research shows that companies who clearly articulate their purpose enjoy higher growth rates than non-for-purpose competitors.

According to Gallup, when it comes to communicating an organization's purpose to your employees, customers, and stakeholders, words don't matter nearly as much as actions do. Companies need to find ways to bring purpose to life. Creating little things that can make a big difference for both employees and customers is one way to bring purpose to life. These little things are called Red Goldfish.

THE PURPOSE ARCHETYPES

The Red Goldfish Project has collected information on over 250 purpose-led companies, specifically looking for ways that brands bring their purpose to life. Our research database includes over 700 articles and nearly 3,500 videos.

In reviewing all of the companies, patterns began to develop. Brands would typically fall into one of eight purpose archetypes. Here are each of the archetypes with an example:

1. The Protector - "Those who protect what is important."

Example: Patagonia - their purpose is to help reimagine a sustainable world for those who come after us.

RED GOLDFISH: GREEN SABBATICALS

One popular Patagonia perk is a program that allows employees to take off up to two months at full pay to do work for environmental groups. In one green sabbatical, Lisa Myers, who works on the company's giving programs, tracked wolves in Yellowstone National Park. "It's easy to go to work when you get paid to do what you love to do," says Myers. Green sabbaticals are clearly about protecting the world for those who come after us and will connect very directly to the people who are in tune with Patagonia products and have a passion for enjoying and protecting our world.

2. The Liberator - "Those who reinvent a broken system."

Example: Harley Davidson - their purpose is to fulfill dreams of personal freedom through the experience of motorcycling.

RED GOLDFISH: FREE RIDING ACADEMY CLASSES

Harley offers free riding academy classes. In 2016, it offered free Riding Academy motorcycle classes for first responders, including firefighters, police, and emergency medical service personnel. The announcement came on the heels of a year-long extension of free rider training for all current and former members of the

US military. Harley's free rider training to military personnel and first responders not only fulfills the "dreams of personal freedom through the experience of motorcycling" of its purpose but also gains appreciation from a broad range of its customers who also value the dedication and sacrifices made by first responders and our military personnel.

3. The Designer - "Those who empower through the creation of revolutionary products."

Example: Apple - their purpose is to make tools for the mind that advance humankind.

RED GOLDFISH: DILLAN'S VOICE

Dillan Barnache was the star of a short film called *Dillan's Voice*. It was created by Apple to celebrate Autism Acceptance Day. The film tells Dillan's story as a nonverbal kid with autism through his own words. His words are typed out on an iPad and then spoken aloud using an augmented and alternative communication (AAC) app. In 2014, when Dillan used his tablet and an AAC app to deliver a moving middle school graduation speech, his use of the technology went viral. Apple is all about the use of its products as life-shifting technology, just as it is for Dillan. In an interview with *Mashable*, Sarah Herrlinger, senior manager for global accessibility policy and initiatives at Apple, said, "For Apple, accessibility is about empowering everyone to use our technology to be creative, productive, and independent."

4. The Guide - "Those who help facilitate individual progress."

Example: Google - their purpose is to organize the world's information and make it universally accessible.

RED GOLDFISH: TGIF

Google is committed to keeping employees up to speed on the state of business and has been since the beginning. One of Google's first and most famous perks is their Friday afternoon business-update-beer-bash named "TGIF." Google's business leaders, and even the founders, gather to deliver in-person business updates to employees. These candid conversations from the mouths of company leaders keep employees connected to the company's goals, challenges, and opportunities, which helps keep them tied to purpose as well. It's noteworthy that TGIF now takes place on Thursdays so employees in Google's Asian offices can dial in for the business update. The concept behind TGIF is to help employees stay in the loop so they can understand where the company is going and can better help it get there, to keep organizing information for everyone to access.

5. The Advocate - "Those who advocate for a tribe."

Example: Panera - their purpose is to help people live consciously and eat deliciously.

RED GOLDFISH: PANERA CARES

Panera Cares community cafes are a 501(c)3 organization to offer a meal to anyone who comes in, regardless of whether they can pay. They operate on a pay-what-you-can model, providing suggested donation amounts for their menu items, but those who cannot pay are fed free. The funds collected cover operating costs but also cover the cost of meals for those who come to eat but who cannot pay or cannot pay the suggested amount. The cafes help raise awareness about the widespread problem of hunger in our own country.

Panera's Red Goldfish feeds those who need food, and enacted a part of their purpose "to help people... eat deliciously."

6. The Challenger - "Those who inspire people toward transformative action."

Example: Nike - their purpose is to inspire every athlete...and if you have a body, you are an athlete.

RED GOLDFISH: NIKE+ RUNNING APP

Nike+ is not just another fitness app. It has an illustrious pedigree dating way back to the glory days of the Steve Jobs era of Apple. The iconic orange swoosh app icon first made its appearance on the iPod in 2006 and was approved by Jobs himself.

7. The Unifier - "Those who command individuals to join a movement."

Example: Whole Foods - their purpose is to set the standards of excellence for food retailers.

RED GOLDFISH: ORGANIC FOOD STANDARDS

Whole Foods' standards aren't standard anywhere else. Every year there's more demand for "sustainable food" and "natural food products." In developing their standards, they research everything from food additives to antibiotics in meat production, sustainable seafood to organic skincare. If you want quality assurance about what goes into the products you buy, their standards make it easy, because if the product doesn't meet their high standards, they don't sell it. There are many definitions out there for "natural food products" and many opinions on what food additives to avoid. Among other criteria, they draw a line when it comes to hydrogenated fats and artificial colors, flavors, preservatives, and sweeteners.

8. The Master - "Those on a mission to change lives and improve the world."

Example: Warby Parker - their purpose is to offer designer eyewear at a revolutionary price while leading the way for socially conscious businesses.

RED GOLDFISH: BUY A PAIR, GIVE A PAIR

Rather than donating the glasses outright, the company makes cash donations from its sales to VisionSpring, a non-profit for which Warby Parker founder Neil Blumenthal used to work. Vision-Spring trains low-income men and women to sell glasses in their communities for affordable prices, allowing them to earn a living. This helps ensure Warby Parker's donations actually meet people's needs and don't displace local businesses. As of 2015, Warby Parker has distributed more than 1 million pairs of glasses through 10,000 emerging market entrepreneurs. By providing cash donations to create products for sustainable jobs for low-income men and women, Warby Parker's Red Goldfish Buy a Pair, Give a Pair fulfills both parts of the company's purpose: "offer designer eyewear at a revolutionary price, while leading the way for socially conscious businesses."

WHAT'S YOUR PURPOSE ARCHETYPE?

Which one of the eight archetypes resonates with your organization? How are you doing the little things to bring your purpose to life? What's your Red Goldfish?

So far we've examined technology and purpose as differentiators. Now, let's examine how our flaws hold the key to what makes us awesome.

CHAPTER 10

WHY PINK?

*"We should be revering, perhaps even illuminating,
the flaws that make us unique—
one of a kind and imperfectly special."*

- Tammy Lenski

Pink became the sixth color in the Goldfish Series in 2018.

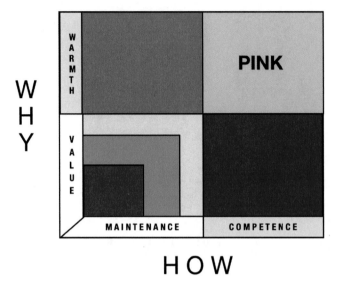

Why pink? Because pink is often associated with differentiation and uniqueness.

Pink was first used as a color name in the late 1600s. The golden age for pink was during the Rococo Period in the 1700s. Pastel colors became fashionable in all of the courts in Europe. Pink was particularly championed by the mistress of Louis XV, Madame de Pompadour.

Throughout the 1800s and into the early 1900s, pink ribbons or decorations were often worn by young boys in England. Boys were considered small men, and while men in England wore red uniforms, boys wore pink. Pink was seen as a more masculine color than blue. For example, a 1918 article in Earnshaw's Infants' Department explained that "the generally accepted rule is pink for the boys and blue for the girls. The reason is that pink, being a more decided and stronger color, is more suitable for the boy, while blue, which is more delicate and dainty, is prettier for the girl." This is the exact opposite of the way we now think about pink.

It wasn't until the mid-1900s that people started choosing pink for girls and blue for boys. This became the accepted norm in the 1940s. The tipping point for pink occurred in 1953 when the new First Lady of the United States, Mamie Eisenhower, wore a pink gown for the presidential inauguration of her husband, Dwight D. Eisenhower.

The biggest reason behind pink is my *Pink Goldfish* co-author. David Rendall is the ultimate advocate for embracing weirdness and exploiting imperfection. David wears head to toe pink on stage. This includes pink pants, pink shoes, pink socks, a pink belt, and a pink watch. His shirts display his trademark pink Tyrannosaurus Rex. He even has a custom-made three-piece pink pinstripe suit, which he wears with a pink shirt, pink tie, and pink Chuck Taylor shoes.

When asked about all the pink, he points to his family as the inspiration. David and his wife, Stephanie, have three daughters named Sophia, Emma, and Anna. Even his dog Snowbell is a female. During his speeches, he tells a series of funny stories about how living in a house full of women who were gradually trying to turn him into a woman. From pushing him to use an exfoliating body wash to painting his toenails, to trimming his eyebrows, the Rendall women were on a mission to make him more like them. Instead of pushing back, David chose to embrace it and the color that it represents—pink.

His unconventional commitment to pink makes him memorable to his audiences. David leaned in and pink has become inextricably linked to his brand.

We use pink as a symbol for embracing weirdness and amplifying weakness. It represents the idea that our flaws make us awesome. To understand this, we must travel back over 600 years ago to Japan.

TALE OF ASHIKAGA YOSHIMASA

In the 15th century, the Japanese Shogun Ashikaga Yoshimasa had a prized favorite tea bowl. Just like you might have a personal favorite coffee mug that's irreplaceable. One day Askikaga mistakenly knocked his tea bowl over and it smashed into pieces. Disheartened, he sent it out to be repaired. When it came back, it was fixed using ugly metal staples and coarse black glue. When Ashikaga held it in his hands his heart sank. This was unacceptable. It spurred him to summon his best craftsman from the entire Osaka region. Ashikaga challenged them to find a more aesthetically pleasing method of repair. The craftsmen carefully took apart the bowl. They meticulously cleaned each broken section. Then, they put it back together using lacquer and gold to repair the cracks. It took them two weeks.

When Ashikaga was presented with the bowl, the shogun was extremely pleased with the result. His heart leapt. The bowl with its golden seams was better now than when it was perfectly normal.

Photo Credit: Shutterstock

Born out of the efforts of these craftsmen came the Japanese art of Kintsugi. It is the practice of repairing broken pottery with lacquer dusted or mixed with powdered gold, silver, or platinum. Kintsugi in Japanese translates to "golden joinery." It is a metaphor for embracing our flaws. Kintsugi espouses the idea that the broken is more beautiful than the pristine. The gold is used to intentionally call attention to the flaws instead of concealing them.

Japanese collectors became so enamored with the new art form. Dealers were accused of deliberately smashing valuable pottery so it could be repaired with the golden seams of kintsugi.

Here is the important takeaway from the art form. Mending the cracks makes the object more beautiful, not despite the flaws, but because of the attention placed on them. This is the crux of the reasoning behind the Pink Goldfish strategy of embracing what makes you weird or weak. In the words of author and speaker Tammy Lenski, we should be "revering, perhaps even illuminating, the flaws that make us unique—one of a kind and imperfectly special."

> "Most of us spend our lives trying to be, and seem, 'perfect.' We try to protect ourselves. It can sometimes be difficult to drop the pretense and own up to your flaws and faults – it takes courage."
>
> - Brené Brown, *The Gifts of Imperfection*

STANDING OUT IN BUSINESS

In her book, *Different: Escaping the Competitive Herd*, Harvard Business School marketing professor Youngme Moon points out that, "the ability to compete is dependent upon the ability to differentiate from competitors."

However, she goes on to say, "The number of companies who are truly able to achieve competitive separation is depressingly small." This is because companies tend to define their strengths and weaknesses using the same measurements and standards as their competitors. This leads to homogeneity, not differentiation. When everyone is trying to build on the same strengths and eliminate the same weaknesses, all companies begin to look the same.

It's very common for brands to homogenize. As we look at what successful companies are doing, it's natural to emulate them. This has even been institutionalized in the process of benchmarking.

We try to find out what others are doing right and then do the same thing. It sounds reasonable, but there's a problem.

The problem is that when everyone in an industry starts copying the leaders, then, over time, the entire industry starts to look the same, feel the same, and sound the same. There are no differences. Nothing distinguishes one brand from another. As Moon explains, "The dynamic is not unlike a popularity contest in which everyone tries to win by being equal parts friendly, happy, active, and fun. Once everyone starts doing it, no one stands out."

So how can you create one of the few organizations that become extraordinary?

First, fitting in and becoming a "me too" brand will never lead to success. Benchmarking is not the path to greatness. Second, trying to fix a weakness is a waste of time and effort. Third, if you try to be great at everything, you will end up being great at nothing. If you try to please everyone, you won't end up pleasing anyone. It is a recipe for mediocrity.

It is good to be different, to stick out, and be unique. It is good to flaunt your weaknesses instead of fixing them. It is good to be un-balanced. Our flaws can hold the keys to what makes us awesome.

However, it can be just as dangerous to simply remain average. Management guru Tom Peters argues that it is no longer safe to be the same, to be normal, to be indistinct. Let that sink in for a minute. He is saying that the only safe move— only prudent choice, the only wise decision— is to become unusual, different, strange, and remark-able. Pink Goldfish is based on the belief that weird brands win.

THE CASE FOR DIFFERENTIATION

A portmanteau is a French word for a small suitcase. It also de-scribes when parts of multiple words are combined to make a new word. For example, by blending smoke and fog to create smog. Or vlog, from video, web, and log. A portmanteau relates to a singular concept that the combined word describes. Our portmanteau for differentiation is FLAWSOME. It is a combination of FLAWS and AWESOME—the simple idea that your flaws hold the key to what makes you awesome in business.

The concept of flawsome isn't new. The term was used by both Trendspotting and the supermodel Tyra Banks. According to Trendspotting in 2012, consumers don't expect brands to be flawless. In fact, consumers will embrace brands that are FLAWSOME:

brands that are still brilliant despite having flaws; even being flawed (and being open about it) can be awesome. According to Tyra Banks, FLAWSOME is used to describe something that is awesome because of its flaws. She advocates for us to embrace the flaws in our bodies and own them for they are simply flawsome. Tyra launched the Flawsome Ball to benefit her TZONE Foundation in 2012.

In addition to the flawsome portmanteau, it is also an acronym. Each letter in the F.L.A.W.S.O.M.E. framework represents one of eight ways to differentiate. The F of FLAWSOME stands for Flaunting. Flaunting is the cornerstone of the framework. According to the *Encarta Dictionary*, flaunt means "to parade without shame." Our interpretation is that flaunting is positive. Flaunting is about being unapologetic about your flaws. You take pride in your organization's unique characteristics. You emphasize them, accentuate them, feature them, highlight them, expose them, and openly display them.

Weird is what makes you different or unique in business. Weird is usually seen as a weakness or a flaw because it doesn't conform to the established model of success. Doing something abnormal is often seen as doing it the "wrong way." Normal represents the standards within your industry. Normal defines the "right way." Normal is usually synonymous with strong. If everyone is doing it, then it must be a good thing. To illustrate this, we created the Flaunting Matrix.

THE FLAUNTING MATRIX

The Flaunting Matrix contains four quadrants, each of which is represented by an animal. The first quadrant, the top left, represents doing less of what makes you weird. It is the **COW** quadrant:

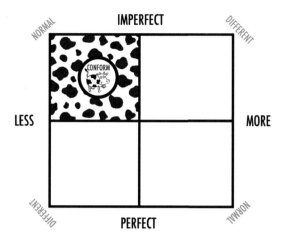

Why a Cow? Every cow is unique. Their spots are like fingerprints. No two cows are alike. Yet, cows are blissfully unaware of their uniqueness. Establish a cowpath and cows will never stray from it.

This is the **CONFORM** quadrant.

The second quadrant, the top right, represents doing more of what makes you weird. It is the **PEACOCK** quadrant:

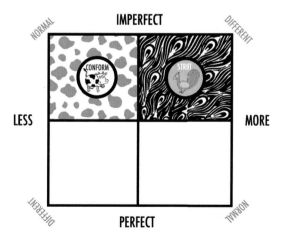

Why a Peacock? Like cows and their spots, the feathers on a peacock are unique. Unlike cows, they own it. Their uniqueness is a signature part of who they are. They purposefully preen and flaunt their feathers to stand out among the flock. This is the **STRUT** quadrant.

The third quadrant, the bottom right, represents doing more of what makes you normal. It is the **ZEBRA** quadrant.

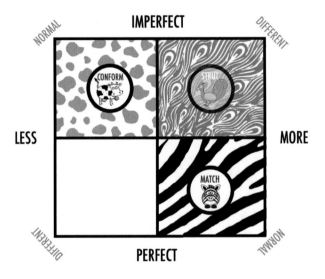

Why a Zebra? Zebras are black with white stripes. Their striping is determined by genetics. Even though zebras are unique, their individual stripes are indistinguishable from other zebras. Their stripes create a blending effect, making it impossible for an individual zebra to stand out among the herd. This is good for safety as predators see the herd as one huge object, but it makes standing out a non-starter. You can't add stripes and be different here. It's just more of the same. This is the **MATCH** quadrant.

The fourth quadrant, the bottom left, represents doing less of what makes you normal. It is the **POLAR BEAR** quadrant:

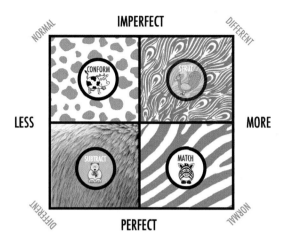

The fourth quadrant in the Flaunting Matrix. Why a Polar Bear? Polar bears aren't white. Their fur is translucent because their individual hair is hollow. The fur absorbs the light and takes away all of the colors in the spectrum so they appear white. Generally, polar bears avoid the herd and live solitary lives. This is the SUBTRACT quadrant of the matrix.

If you want to stand out, you need to be like a peacock and a polar bear.

EIGHT TYPES OF PINK GOLDFISH

In our research of nearly 400 highly differentiated brands, we've found there are eight different types of Pink Goldfish. They follow the acronym of FLAWSOME.

Flaunting is the cornerstone of the FLAWSOME framework. The remaining seven types are Lopsiding, Antagonizing, Withholding, Swerving, Opposing, Micro-weirding, and Exposing. Let's have a look at each beginning with Lopsiding.

Lopsiding involves amplifying, not reducing, your brand's flaws. The approach is to expand them, magnify them, turn them up, exaggerate them, and then supersize them.

Example: Established in 1919, W.K. Buckley formulated a cough syrup called Buckley's Mixture. Noted for its strongly unpleasant taste, the Canadian cough syrup is not for the faint of heart. The company decided to lopside the flaw and began promoting a new slogan for the brand, "It tastes awful. And it works." The "bad taste" campaign increased Buckley's market share by over 550 percent in the Canadian cough & cold category.

Antagonizing is about polarizing, repelling, and taunting. It's based on the realization that if you try to be for everyone... you end up being for no one. It advocates for alienating your non-target market. The more some people hate you, the more others will love you.

Example: The Alamo Drafthouse once received a nasty voicemail from a customer. She complained about being thrown out for violating their strict no-talking, no-texting policy. Instead of apologizing, they made her voicemail into a Public Service Announcement they play in the previews.

Withholding is about consciously doing less of what everyone else considers normal. This is an anti-benchmarking strategy.

Example: How do you compete on Black Friday? Longer hours and bigger sales. REI decided against both and closed their stores on the biggest day in retail. The result: they gained memberships and sales increased.

Swerving is the "S" in FLAWSOME. I am not going to tell you what it is. In fact, I'm going to withhold and flaunt the fact. And, I hope it antagonizes a few of you reading this.

Opposing is doing the exact opposite of what others are doing. Opposing brands are unlike other brands. They are contradictory, dissimilar. They operate in a way that is incompatible with everyone else. Opposing involves defying, resisting, and fighting.

Example: Normal socks are sold in pairs. Each sock in the pair matches the other one. That is how socks work. Yet, Little Miss-matched sells socks in sets of three. Also, they sell socks that don't match and they do it on purpose.

Micro-weirding is using minuscule actions to differentiate your brand. The lesson is that you can set your brand apart without some cohesive master plan; you can be just a tiny bit weird.

Example: It will cost you to be stupid at Tom's. Tom's Diner in Denver, Colorado was founded by Tom Messina in 1999. They became the focus of international attention in January of 2020 when their $.38 charge for stupid questions went viral on social media. This wasn't a random one-time decision by a server or cashier. The cost of a stupid question is listed on the menu.

Exposing is the eighth and final type in the FLAWSOME framework. Exposing is about honesty, transparency, and authenticity. In order to expose, you have to be willing to reveal, instead of conceal; declare, instead of deny; disclose, instead of disguise; confide, instead of hide.

Example: Snowbird exposes one-star reviews like "Too Advanced" and "Disappointed." These one-star reviews were part of a marketing campaign by Snowbird. The mountain resort in Utah knows that they are not for every skier and snowboarder. The trails at the mountain are difficult. Some may see that as a flaw or weakness, but it's a badge they wear with pride.

It's easy to follow the crowd. It feels safe. But it's not. Successful brands stick out. They are unusual. Don't apologize for your flaws and don't try to fix them. Instead, exploit your brand's imperfections. You can't make everyone happy. So don't try. Choose whom you will reject. Decide whom you will repel. Do it deliberately.

The colors pink, red, and blue occupy the middle of the Black Matrix. Next, we'll look at the top-level elements of connection and progress.

CHAPTER 11

CONNECTION AND PROGRESS

*"Coming together is a beginning;
keeping together is progress;
working together is success."*

- Edward Everett Hale

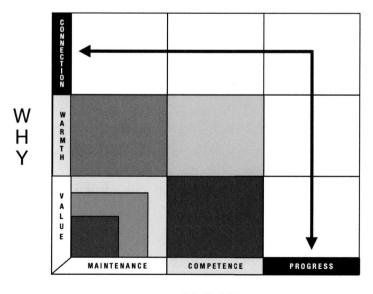

A recent global study by Lippincott of more than 400 brands uncovered how winning brands outperform the competition. They do it by leveraging "meaning" in business.

Meaning is defined as coming from two sources:

1. Connection - the kind that drives personal value
2. Progress - the kind that drives action

Beyond warmth and competence, these are next-level concepts.

DEFINING CONNECTION AND PROGRESS

Let's look at both connection and progress. Each element is defined by two factors:

Connection

1. Understanding the customer as an individual. You demonstrate that you share their values and aspirations.
2. Actively demonstrating that you care. You focus on creating value for the customer and have their best interests at heart.

Progress

1. Managing expectations of how things should work and putting the customer in control. You design elegant solutions that achieve the most effective outcome with minimal customer effort.
2. Committing to solve the big problems that your customers face. Allowing you to communicate and connect meaningfully with others who have the same quest.

BUILDING BRANDS IN A HARSH NEW WORLD

Creating a strongly differentiated brand these days isn't cheap or easy. There are few barriers to entry and past performance is no guarantee of future results. Shifts in markets, technology, and society are making it tougher than ever to stand out in the marketplace.

Getting to this higher level of connection and progress comes less from what you do. It comes from why and how you do it.

- How can you help your customers with what they are struggling to achieve?
- How can you reduce the pressure they feel?
- How can you communicate in a way that's purposeful and clear to drive a deeper connection and happiness?
- How can you connect across the generations?

Let's look at four ways to build connection and progress starting with happiness.

CHAPTER 12

WHY YELLOW?

"[Gezellig] It stands for something or someone cozy, nice, homey, friendly, snuggly, fun, comfortable or enjoyable... but no word can really sum it all up. It's a feeling rather than a word."

- Shoshannah Hausmann

Yellow became the seventh color in the Goldfish Series in 2018.

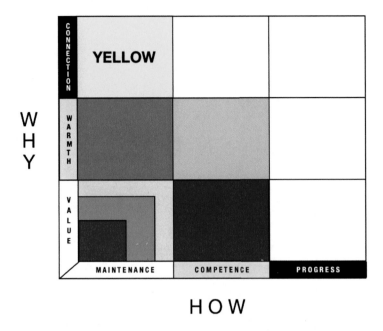

Why yellow? There are two reasons yellow represents happiness and connection.

First, yellow is the brightest and most cheerful of all the colors in the spectrum. As a color specialist and the executive director of the Pantone Color Institute, Leatrice Eiseman has conducted various color word-association studies on thousands of people over the last 30 years. She has found that the first words that consistently come to mind when people see the color yellow are "warmth," "cheer," "happiness," and sometimes even "playfulness."

Why do we have these warm and positive feelings about yellow?

It's because we associate yellow with the sun. Interestingly, the sun is actually white. We perceive it as yellow because of the higher wavelength of the color. Yellow is scattered less easily by Earth's atmosphere, leaving the color for us to see. Blue, on the other hand, has low wavelengths, which explains why it is strewn across the sky. Because yellow is the lightest hue of the spectrum, the color is uplifting and illuminating. It offers hope, happiness, and fun.

Another reason for yellow is from the round smiley happy face created by the late graphic artist Harvey Ross Ball.

According to the *Smithsonian,* Ball was engaged by State Mutual Life Assurance Company of Worcester, Massachusetts, to create a happy face. State Mutual wanted to raise the morale of the employees. Ball's iconic graphic involved a bright yellow background, dark oval eyes, a full smile, and creases at the sides of the mouth. It took 10 minutes to create the smiley face and Ball was paid 45 dollars for the graphic.

Over the next half-century, versions of the smiley face would be imprinted on more than fifty million buttons and became popular around the world. It has become an icon for happiness and is responsible for spawning the development of digital emoticons.

A WORD WORTH TRAVELING TO THE NETHERLANDS TO GET

In 2000, I moved to Amsterdam for my job with adidas. During my first few months of living in the city, I experienced the friendliness of the Dutch and their easy-going nature. The Dutch tend to be happy people. In fact, according to a recent *Happiness Report,* the country is the fifth happiest country in the world out of 156.

I thoroughly enjoyed hanging out with both expats and my new local Dutch friends. It wasn't long before I heard a strange word being frequently uttered by both groups. That word was "gezellig."

The Middle Dutch word is pronounced *heh-sell-ick* with an emphasis on the guttural Dutch "g" in the first and third syllables. It's hard to define this widely used word as it has a variety of meanings. It's more like a feeling.

According to *Wikipedia*:

> Gezellig is a Dutch word which, depending on the context, can be translated as conviviality, coziness, and fun. It is often used to describe a social and relaxed situation. It can also indicate belonging, time spent with loved ones, catching up with an old friend or just the general togetherness that gives people a warm feeling. A common trait to all descriptions of *gezellig* is a general and abstract sensation of individual well-being that one typically shares with others. All descriptions involve a positive atmosphere, flow or vibe that colors the individual personal experience in a favorable way and in one way or another corresponds to social contexts.

Gezellig is the word that most aptly describes a Yellow Goldfish. Yellow Goldfish are the positive things we do when creating an experience. Experiences that generate happiness for employees, customers, and society. Small things that create a moment and distinct feeling of connection.

Like the word lagniappe, gezellig would stick with me.

I am also indebted to The Netherlands for a couple more reasons.

In late 2000, I had a chance encounter at Schiphol Airport in Amsterdam. I approached a woman at baggage claim after a redeye flight from New York.

"Excuse me, this is going to sound like a horrible pickup line, but I think I know you?"

She quickly looked me up and down, "No."

Unfazed, I pressed on. "Do you live here in Amsterdam?" Another quick "No" in response.

"Do you live in New York City?" I asked. I had moved from Manhattan earlier in the year. "No."

I felt like her patience was beginning to wear thin. After a quick no to Portland, Oregon I asked in retreat, "OK, where do you live?"

She replied, "I live in Connecticut." The lightbulb went off. I smiled and said, "Jennifer Wills... we went to High School together."

Four years later she would become my wife.

In 2017, I connected with Rosaria Louwman on social media. Born and raised in Italy, Rosaria and I bonded quickly on the importance of happiness in business. She lives just outside of Amsterdam. In short order, we teamed up to explore the concept of a Yellow Goldfish.

HAPPINESS IS THE ULTIMATE WHY

We found that happiness relates to our "Why" as human beings and to our common goal as a living species. Aristotle pointed out that if we apply "why" to any question, at the end we find that everything we do relates to wanting to be and feel happier. In his words: "Happiness is something final and self-sufficient, and is the end of action. Everything that we choose, we choose for the sake of something else—except happiness."

Happiness can be the most sustainable competitive advantage and the ultimate currency in business. It offers a competitive advantage because we buy, work, and live to pursue and attain happiness; because we buy more, work better and more effectively, and live longer and healthier lives when we are happy.

We are at the beginning of a widespread realization that there is a 5.0 version of business that sees happiness at the center of what we do. Happiness for the customers that we serve, happiness of the employees within the organization, happiness at a societal level, and happiness for the next generation.

When happiness is at the center and everything else rotates with purpose around it, profit, prosperity, and growth will follow as a result.

WHY HAPPINESS IN BUSINESS

Happiness is becoming the new competitive advantage. Happy customers and happy employees drive healthy growth—even in a time of crisis. Why? Happiness matters in business along three dimensions:

1. Employees: Happy employees have the highest return on investment (ROI) because they:

   - are more productive, creative, and innovative.

   - have lower sickness, absenteeism, and turnover rates—thereby reducing bottom-line expenses.

   - provide valuable feedback for improvement because they care more about their company.

   - deliver the best service to customers because they are happy themselves.

2. Customers: Happy customers are most profitable because they:

   - buy more and are willing to pay a premium price.

   - remain customers over the long term.

   - are more likely to forgive a mistake and have a lower cost to serve.

- give you their most valuable asset—TIME—by providing valuable feedback for improvement, writing reviews, and engaging in your communities/forums.

3. Society/Community: Happy citizens bring substantial benefits for society as a whole. The article *"Happiness and Psychological Well-Being: Building Human Capital to Benefit Individuals and Society"* in *The Solutions Journal* summarizes the benefits. Happy citizens:

- are healthy people, live longer and enjoy a greater quality of life.

- function at a higher level, utilizing their personal strengths, skills, and abilities to contribute to their own well-being as well as that of others and society.

- are more likely to be compassionate and, therefore, to contribute to the moral fiber of society in diversely beneficial ways.

- are less prone to experience depression and, if they do, tend to manage it better and more quickly. They are less likely to experience anxiety, stress, or anger.

Happiness is a feeling, but it's also about perception. Perception and feeling are the cornerstones of both customer and employee experience.

How can you design and deliver experiences that delight customers, employees, and society overall? Our goal was to answer that question through the Yellow Goldfish Project.

Using the data collected from the 300 companies we researched, Rosaria and I specifically looked for ways that brands can enhance happiness in business. In reviewing all of the companies, we began to see patterns. We saw that brands could leverage nine different ways to drive happiness for customers, employees, and society.

The nine ways make the acronym of H.A.P.P.I.N.E.S.S:

H is for Health – It all starts with Health. Without health, we have nothing in life, and happiness is a non-starter. It's an easy concept to grasp. You need to manage your health as a basic need to achieve a state of wellness.

Example: The Max Borges Agency offers its employees benefits such as an onsite gym, fitness classes, and reimbursement for athletic competition entry fees.

A is for Autonomy – Autonomy is about having control over both work and life. Freedom and control over one's actions promotes happiness.

Example: Patagonia employees enjoy what the company calls "Let My People Go Surfing" time, a period during any workday where employees can head outdoors to get their creative juices flowing. Of course, they can't abandon their duties or ditch a meeting, but popping out for an impromptu climb or bike ride is encouraged.

P is for Purpose – According to Gallup, when it comes to communicating an organization's purpose to your employees, customers, and stakeholders, words don't matter nearly as much as actions do. Companies need to find ways to bring purpose to life to promote happiness.

Example: Greyston Bakery runs The Center for Open Hiring. It is a collaborative learning space that helps to facilitate the widespread adoption of Open Hiring and supports innovation in the delivery of community programs for employees and neighbors.

P is for Play – Engaging in play triggers all of the DOSE chemicals in the brain that influences our happiness (DOSE: Dopamine, Oxytocin, Serotonin, Endorphins).

Example: Southwest Airlines' funny flight safety announcements inject fun, creativity, and recognition into everyday experiences to increase happiness and loyalty.

I is for Integrity – Integrity is about operating your business in an honest way that everyone can believe in.

Example: Tony Chocolonely exists to change the chocolate industry by making 100 percent slave-free production the norm. They are out to show that chocolate can be made with integrity, through direct relationships with cocoa farmers and other supply chain partners.

N is for Nature – Nature and strong design can be a powerful resource to us in creating happier and healthier lives.

Example: Doug Dietz of GE Healthcare created an MRI scanner experience that not only didn't frighten children but provided them with an adventure.

E is for Empathy - Feeling connected to other people is at the heart of happiness. All existing research on happiness confirms that the quality of relationships with the people we care about and surround ourselves with is the number one predictor of Happiness.

Example: The Lexus brand has the strong influence of Japanese omotenashi in every aspect of its business. Lexus dealers always treat customers as they would a guest in their own home, going to any lengths to solve their automotive problems, mechanical or otherwise.

S is for Simplicity - The more you can cut, the more efficient you can be in conveying your message or designing an experience that creates happiness.

Example: The drive to simplify would become the hallmark of the Apple brand. "It takes a lot of hard work," the late Steve Jobs said, "to make something simple, to truly understand the underlying challenges and come up with elegant solutions." As the headline of Apple's first marketing brochure proclaimed in 1977, "Simplicity is the ultimate sophistication."

S is for Smile - When we smile, we send a message to the body to rebalance, to cultivate health, vitality, and inner joy.

Example: Qualtrics offers its employees a chance to fulfill a personal dream. This new benefit called the "Dream Experience" is for full-time employees who have been at the company for at least one year. Each employee receives $1,500 to create a unique experience.

It is important to stand out and differentiate. Happiness offers a competitive advantage because we buy, work, and live to pursue and attain happiness; because we buy *more*, work *better and more effectively*, and live *longer and healthier* lives when we are happy.

We can choose where to focus in business. Choose happiness.

If happiness helps drive connection, our next color is focused on progress through leadership.

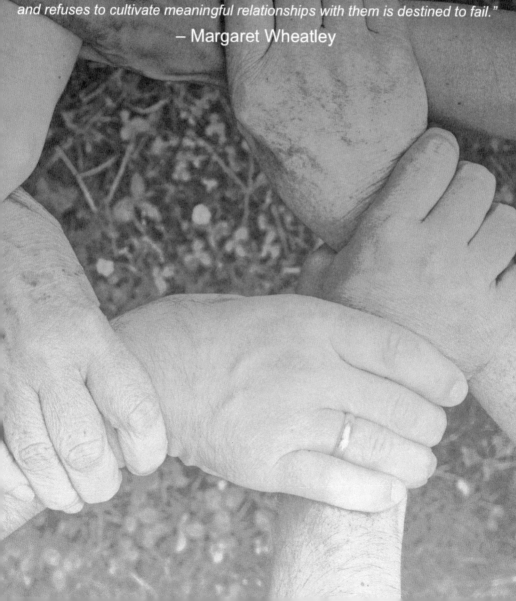

CHAPTER 13

WHY GRAY?

*"There is only one prediction about the future that I feel confident to make.
During this period of random and unpredictable change,
any organization that distances itself from its employees
and refuses to cultivate meaningful relationships with them is destined to fail."*

– Margaret Wheatley

Gray became the eighth color in the Goldfish Series in 2019.

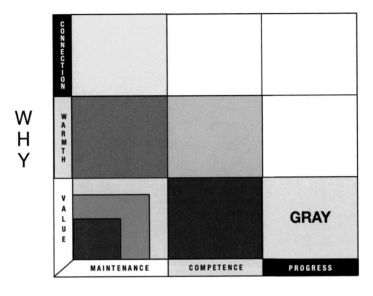

Why gray? Gray represents the idea that there is no black and white approach to leadership. That there isn't always a clear-cut path to becoming a great leader. In fact, there seldom is. When you couple this with leading people who, because of their generation, perceive the world very differently. You have to use a variety of techniques to overcome challenges and get the most from your employees. A one-size-fits-all approach is a recipe for disaster because your employees approach their work differently. This holds true even for an organization with just one generation, much less one with five. You are going to have to navigate plenty of gray areas to find the approach that works best.

Gray is a color often associated with something nondescript or unremarkable. I hate to be the one to tell you this, but that's how most employees view their leadership teams. *Forbes* revealed that 63 percent of employees don't trust their leaders. Gallup also completed a study saying a staggering 87 percent of employees are not engaged (and leadership plays at least a passing role in that). In addition, Accor/Edenred states that 90 percent of companies think an engagement strategy will improve business success. Yet, very few companies have a strategy. Is it because they don't want to be successful? Perhaps they're too lazy? Or maybe it's because they don't know how.

A NEW BALLGAME

In preparation for the 2018 season, the Phillies, Mets, Red Sox, Yankees, and the Nationals all replaced veteran managers with younger skippers. The differences in age were marked. The five managers ranged from 8 to 26 years younger than their predecessors. Some had no major league managing experience. According to Tom Verducci of *Sports Illustrated*, "the ability to connect with young players and a comfort with analytics rose above experience." These new managers were better at relating to the latest generation of players. One of them was 42-year-old Alex Cora who led the Boston Red Sox to a World Series title in his first year at the helm. This move by traditionally conservative baseball owners should be a wake-up call for today's leaders.

FIVE GENERATIONS

With the introduction of Generation Z (born starting in 1997) into the workplace, we now have an unprecedented five generations at work. Generation Z joins the largest group, Millennials, followed by Generation X, Baby Boomers, and Matures. It is not uncommon for today's leaders to have team members that span 50 years from oldest to youngest. Speaking from experience, my father-in-law, Fred Wills worked three days a week for the Town of Shelton, Connecticut until he was 89.

The ability to relate and connect across these generations is vital. Each of the five generations brings its own unique expectations and needs. Sticking with our initial theme of baseball, Angels manager Joe Maddon believes that effective leadership and culture start with relationships. Strong relationships lead to trust and trust leads to the willingness to exchange thoughts and ideas. That foundation breeds success and progress.

For today's leaders, the idea of managing teams that include five different generations is new territory. According to Carol Hymowitz in the *Wall Street Journal*, "That means they must create opportunities for young employees to advance (or risk losing them) while also making sure veterans, whose skills they need in today's tight labor market, don't feel overlooked. And to maintain productivity and innovation, they must persuade employees of disparate ages to collaborate." They must effectively navigate the gray.

> *"Friction and misunderstandings often occur when communicating across generations. It gets even more challenging when working across virtual settings."*
>
> – Raymond Arroyo

EVERYONE IS STRUGGLING WITH GENERATIONAL DIFFERENCES

There was one story that inspired *Gray Goldfish*. It came from my coauthor Brian Doyle during his time working in financial services.

It began in a conference room. As the business's President was wrapping up his latest story, Brian looked at the empty seat next to him. The meeting was supposed to have started five minutes ago and his sales analyst wasn't here yet. Then he heard it. It was faint at first.

Flip, flop, flip, flop, flip flop.

Brian could tell by the frequency of the flipping and flopping that his 25-year-old sales analyst in sandals knew she was late. She entered the room with a stack of papers to hand to the attendees and wearing a skirt that was a little shorter than what he usually saw at work. Though Brian saw no reaction from his male counterparts, he could see some of the women's faces cloud with disapproval. His sales analyst Blair sat in the open chair between him and the President. As the President finished his story to mild laughter around the room, Blair laughed and said, "Oh, great story, Dave! Should we get started?"

Complimenting the President and getting the meeting started without further delay was exactly the right thing to do. But when Brian stole a quick glance at the senior leaders around the room, he didn't see any appreciation for Blair taking the initiative. Instead, he saw a group of irritated forty and fifty-year-olds. Each of them worked hard to be a direct report to the President, and they weren't very happy to see one of the business's youngest employees getting the spotlight.

Blair proceeded to walk through an extremely insightful analysis. Her report clearly showed where the sales force was succeeding and where it was failing. It also provided leads for reps to call on for new business. She was confident and articulate in her presentation—highlighting aspects of the analysis to the various leaders in the room. As she used their first names to direct their attention to a particular part of the report, the leaders would slowly lean back in their chairs and fold their arms. Their body language was sending a message—either they didn't like the presentation or they didn't like Blair. When she concluded her talk there was silence.

After a few moments that screamed "Awk–ward!" Brian asked, "So what do you all think?" A few grumbled "nice work" but that was it.

The President continued the agenda and eventually concluded the meeting.

Then the parade began when Brian got back to his office.

"What the hell was she thinking?" one sales leader started. "She shows up late, acts like she owns the place, and then tries to monopolize the entire meeting. I tried to help her out by asking a question, and she responded like she was my friend. I've been paying my dues here for 25 years—how dare she act like she's my equal. She should have shown it to me before the meeting, so I could make some intelligent comments in front of the President."

The next few senior leaders through my doorway said essentially the same thing. "You need to rein her in" and, "She thinks she should be CEO tomorrow, and she's only been here a year."

Just when Brian thought the day's venting was over, Blair came into his office.

She was just as frustrated as her older counterparts, but for different reasons. "What the hell were they thinking? I've been busting my butt on this analysis for an entire week. "I got no feedback and no thanks for my work. This is the sort of thing that should get me promoted and instead it's like it's totally worthless. They're just intimidated because I'm young and have new ideas."

In the end, the older generation of senior leaders around that table was right ... and wrong. And so was Blair. It came down to perspective—a perspective driven by their generation. The Baby Boomers and Generation Xers who represented the company's leadership team were raised in a totally different environment and with parents who used completely different parenting techniques than Blair, as a Millennial, was accustomed to. Right then Brian realized that he needed to get a better understanding of each generation.

UNDERSTANDING THE FIVE GENERATIONS

In order to lead each of the generations, it's important to understand why each generation is the way it is. In other words, what's shaped their attitudes, approaches, and perspectives?

Matures (Born prior to 1946)
Matures about doing their job, taking care of business, and not complaining. Why? The Matures lived through the worst economic times this country has ever seen during the Great Depression. Matures were shaped by an era that required selflessness and sacrifice. It was about a team working together to achieve a common goal.

Matures in one word: **DUTY**

Baby Boomers (Born between 1946 – 1964)
Boomers grew up in an era of abundance. Known as the "Decade of Prosperity," the U.S. economy grew 37 percent in the 1950s. Unemployment dropped as low as 4.5 percent. Boomers pride themselves on achievements. While results are important, it's the process and the dues that have been paid that produced those results that are most important. Defined by their work, Boomers don't mind staying late (even if it means sacrificing some family time), and they take advantage of the opportunity to show off that work ethic to their managers and coworkers. Staying late and working hard are badges of honor for Boomers

Baby Boomers in one word: **WORK**

Generation X (Born between 1965-1979)
Divorce and job security shaped Generation X. Dubbed the latch key kids, they saw divorce spike to nearly 50 percent. From an early age, Gen Xers learned to rely on themselves. They needed to create their own fun and take greater responsibility for their own well-being. They not only saw the need to look out for themselves at home,

they also started to see the need to look out for themselves at work as employment became less stable. Unlike previous generations, late Baby Boomers and Gen Xers saw lifelong employment with the same company end. By the end of 1982, unemployment reached nearly 11 percent—the highest since 1941. In addition to questioning authority, Generation X was also the first generation to mix fun in business in earnest, and they made it known that they cared about their lives outside of work.

Generation X in one word: **BALANCE**

Millennials (Born between 1980 – 1996)
The personalities of the millennial generation were developed in a period of ever-increasing spending. This sort of spending by their parents made Millennials expect more from their new parent figures (their college professors and their managers at work). From an early age, Millennials were told they were special by their overly involved parents. That, if they put their mind to it, they could be anything they wanted to be. Instead of ignoring their children or patting them on the head and telling them "now go and play," the parents of Millennials were (and in many cases, still are) in nearly constant contact with their children.

Millennials in one word: **SPECIAL**

Generation Z (Born after 1996)
While Millennials were raised believing anything was possible, the generation that followed them, Generation Z, saw the results of a market collapse and a struggling economy and that produced lower expectations and even less desire to make a commitment, especially to an employer. Gen Z also sees work commitment as a two-way street; if companies aren't willing to commit to their employment, why should they commit to a company? They don't want to be micromanaged. In truth, no generation really appreciated that, and the Baby Boomers

were the last to tolerate it. Gen Z, however, does realize they don't know everything. Instead of a manager, they want a mentor.

Generation Z in one word: **INTEGRATION**

GRAY GENERATIONAL MATRIX

The following Generational Matrix is going to provide you with clear, actionable approaches to win over and engage every generation in your workforce, so you can create a strategy specific to your employees and your situation.

As you see in the figure below, the five generations of leaders are listed across the top. Simply find your generation and then move down the page to find the generation you're leading. Within each cell, you'll see four quick tips on how to recruit, train, manage, and inspire that particular generation.

GRAY GOLDFISH

EMPLOYEES

🐟 **MATURES** BORN PRIOR TO 1946	**BOOMERS** BORN 1946 - 1964
MATURES RECRUIT: Schedule flexibility TRAIN: Classroom MANAGE: Enlist them to train others INSPIRE: Share experiences	RECRUIT: Company integrity TRAIN: Facts & figures MANAGE: Explain how projects help others INSPIRE: Emphasize team
BOOMERS RECRUIT: Status they'll have in the organization TRAIN: Full of information MANAGE: Provide face time to senior leaders INSPIRE: Share keys to climbing ladder	RECRUIT: Team-oriented business TRAIN: Workshops MANAGE: Highlight team successes INSPIRE: Show how work helps community
GEN X RECRUIT: Share that ideas will be respected TRAIN: Summarize, then detail MANAGE: Understand the challenges INSPIRE: Provide autonomy	RECRUIT: Promotion opportunities TRAIN: Interactive MANAGE: Don't micromanage INSPIRE: Earn time off
MILLENNIALS RECRUIT: Opportunity for mentoring TRAIN: Let them practice MANAGE: Assign small projects first INSPIRE: Offer path to promotion	RECRUIT: Appeal to their parents TRAIN: After-training mentors MANAGE: Be open to new ideas INSPIRE: Get to know them
GEN Z RECRUIT: Highlight your culture TRAIN: Bi-directional mentoring MANAGE: Allow worktime flexibility INSPIRE: Listen to their tech ideas	RECRUIT: Speak to brand purpose TRAIN: Mentor, without all the detail MANAGE: Let them work start to finish INSPIRE: Continuous learning

GENERATIONAL MATRIX
LEADERS

GENERATION X BORN 1965 - 1979	MILLENNIALS BORN 1980 - 1996	GENERATION Z BORN 1997 AND AFTER
RECRUIT: Show organizational commitment to being #1 **TRAIN:** Summarize **MANAGE:** Be decisive **INSPIRE:** Explain how you'll win	**RECRUIT:** Value their experience **TRAIN:** Patience **MANAGE:** Spell out what's expected **INSPIRE:** Ask for their input	**RECRUIT:** Alleviate fear of tech **TRAIN:** Explain every step **MANAGE:** Don't count on evenings **INSPIRE:** Show you're working hard too
RECRUIT: Opportunity to shine **TRAIN:** At-your-own-pace **MANAGE:** Allow autonomy **INSPIRE:** Provide details of your plan	**RECRUIT:** Respect past achievements **TRAIN:** Interactive team building **MANAGE:** Share all the credit **INSPIRE:** Help them learn	**RECRUIT:** Show they'll be leading edge **TRAIN:** Focus on soft skills **MANAGE:** Ask them to stay late for big projects **INSPIRE:** Ask for their perspective
RECRUIT: Show how organization is different from others **TRAIN:** Computer-based **MANAGE:** Do your share of the work **INSPIRE:** Work/life balance	**RECRUIT:** Opportunity to do different things **TRAIN:** Role play **MANAGE:** Try to make work easier **INSPIRE:** Fun at work	**RECRUIT:** Highlight lack of bureaucracy **TRAIN:** Self-directed **MANAGE:** Specific goals **INSPIRE:** Give them credit
RECRUIT: Flexible scheduling **TRAIN:** Online **MANAGE:** Check in often **INSPIRE:** Explain importance of work	**RECRUIT:** What you like about the organization **TRAIN:** Multi-tasking interaction **MANAGE:** Celebrate small successes **INSPIRE:** Positive feedback	**RECRUIT:** Highlight your tech **TRAIN:** Connect them with their peers **MANAGE:** Face-to-face feedback **INSPIRE:** Schedule flexibility
RECRUIT: Use tech to communicate **TRAIN:** Mentor, don't tell **MANAGE:** Guide in small steps **INSPIRE:** Customize feedback	**RECRUIT:** Wide use of tech **TRAIN:** Collaboratively and with technology **MANAGE:** Enable work/life integration **INSPIRE:** Explain "why"	**RECRUIT:** Promote diversity **TRAIN:** Gamification **MANAGE:** Leverage tech to simplify **INSPIRE:** Tie work to greater purpose

In order to lead every generation, you need to know how to lead *in the context* of your own generation. That means understanding your own tendencies and the tendencies of those you follow. Regardless of your leadership role, you follow someone. You need to become your leader's favorite employee. Understand the importance of following and helping your manager be the best leader he/she can be. You can also use the matrix in reverse order to coach your manager by finding your generation from the employee side of the matrix and then moving right until you find your manager's generation.

Once you are able to lead across the generations, the next level of progress involves managing yourself and others under pressure.

CHAPTER 14

WHY DIAMOND?

*"You can't problem solve unless you have the ability
or the empathy to perceive all that's around you.
The more you understand what the problem is through other people's lens,
the more you can solve for people, in life, and in business."*

- Andre Agassi

Diamond became the ninth color in the Goldfish Series in 2020.

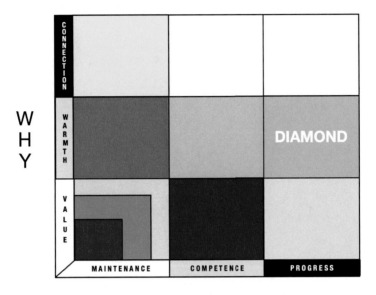

Why diamond? Diamonds are symbolic of pressure. To quote Henry Kissinger, "A diamond is a chunk of coal that did well under pressure." Diamonds are extremely valuable. You won't just find them lying around ready to pick up. You have to go searching for them and you have to uncover where they are hidden.

Diamonds are mined 90 percent less than gold annually. And compared to Platinum, if they maintain clarity and are cut correctly, they can be upwards of 10 times more valuable.

A diamond also symbolizes the best future approach to achieving prosperity and progress in business. Acting in accordance with the Diamond Rule is the next evolution of managing relationships. It's the 4.0 version of winning in sales and client management.

Let's look at 1.0, 2.0, and the 3.0 versions to understand the progression:

Version 1.0 - The Silver Rule

The Silver Rule is "do no harm." As stated by Zigong, a disciple of Confucius, in the book *Analects*, "What I do not wish others to do unto me, I also wish not to do unto others." The problem with Silver is that it's not prescriptive. It doesn't tell you how to treat others. It merely shares what not to do. But as a foundation, it's not a bad start.

FOUNDATIONAL

CASE IN POINT:

Beginning in 2000, Google famously coined "Don't be evil" as part of its code of conduct.

Version 2.0 - The Golden Rule

Throughout nearly every culture and religion, the Golden Rule has become [no pun intended] the gold standard of human dynamics. The Golden Rule is simply "treating others the way you would like to be treated." From a moral perspective, this approach seems reasonable. It can represent the baseline perspective for raising and teaching children.

If the Silver Rule deals in what not to do, the Golden Rule broadens it to all situations. In 2015 with the founding of Alphabet, Google revised its motto of "Don't be evil" to "Do the right thing— follow the law, act honorably, and treat each other with respect." This approach by Google is more aligned with the Golden Rule.

Unfortunately, in sales and managing relationships, the Golden Rule is a bad rule.

Here's why: In most sales organizations, an acceptable conversion rate is about 25 percent, which means that only one out of every four opportunities converts into a sale. Because you were taught to follow the Golden Rule, it's fair to assume you know what your clients want based on what you would want if you were them. Unfortunately, just looking at the conversion rates tells us that there's an issue. If anything else in our businesses was failing 75 percent of the time, we would immediately look for ways to improve.

The Golden Rule can lead to suboptimal results. This is because not everybody wants the same thing or to be treated the same way. We always assume that if something is good for us then it must be good for everyone else. And, that if we want to be treated in a certain way, then that must be how everyone else wants to be treated. Turns out, that assumption couldn't be further from the truth. It leads to failed sales opportunities all the time!

Version 3.0 - The Platinum Rule

The next level of the Golden Rule was popularized by Dr. Tony Alessandra in 1996. It is defined as "treating others the way that they want to be treated." Grounded in emotional intelligence, the Platinum Rule asks you to accommodate the feelings of others.

Dave Kerpen outlines the shortcomings of the Golden Rule in his book *The Art of People.* Kerpen writes, "The Golden Rule, as great as it is, has limitations since all people and all situations are different. When you follow the Platinum Rule, however, you can be sure you're actually doing what the other person wants to be done and assure yourself of a better outcome."

The Platinum Rule is more outward-facing in its approach. The focus shifts from "this is what I want, so I'll give everyone the same thing" to "let me first understand what they want... and then I'll give it to them."

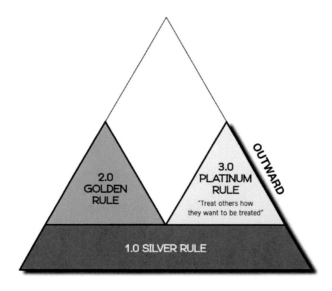

One of the challenges when completely focusing on the other person is that we can overlook how we're feeling and reacting to a situation. For example, we may go into a meeting with the best of intentions to apply the Platinum Rule, but then something happens where we feel upset or disrespected or unheard, and then our capability to actually apply the Platinum Rule is interrupted. Therefore, while the Platinum Rule is aspirational, we must also be true to ourselves and neutralize our biology in order to be capable of addressing the needs of others.

When you play the game of business by following the Platinum Rule, every game is an away game. You never have the home field advantage because success in the game is filtered through the needs and concerns of the other person. Your playbook focuses only on knowing how others want to be treated and what's important to them.

Version 4.0 - The Diamond Rule

The Diamond Rule takes the Platinum Rule to the next level. The key here is understanding both our own biology as well as that of our prospects or customers. Treating someone the way they want to be treated is tricky enough under normal circumstances—but what happens when things start to get heated? In the immortal words of former boxing heavyweight champion Mike Tyson, "Everyone has a plan until they get punched in the mouth." Pressure can trigger a biological response that causes us to act in an unpredictable and irrational manner. Under pressure, our brain activates a hard-wired survival strategy every time it detects a perceived threat.

Why is the Diamond Rule so critical in sales and managing relationships?

The answer is simple. A sales situation is inherently full of pressure. Pressure can make things unstable. In sales, you need to manage yourself and your prospect/client through these difficult situations. The Diamond Rule combines elements of both Gold and Platinum.

Said simply, the Diamond Rule is "the art of managing yourself under pressure and addressing the needs of others to avoid their triggers."

Rooted in the understanding of our own behavioral style and the style of others, the Diamond Rule allows you to solve problems and achieve prosperity in the pressure-filled game of business.

Practicing the Diamond Rule requires two elements: 1) you have to see your own predictable behavioral style when pressure hits, and 2) you need the capability to assess prospects/clients relative to four different, predictable behavioral styles based primarily on how people respond biologically to pressure.

Since we all tend to be pretty strong in only one of the four behavioral styles, it's no surprise that we tend to connect with those whose style is similar to ours but find ourselves challenged to connect with those who have a different style. Therefore, when working outside of our own category, we may be less effective, leading to upwards of a 75 percent failure rate in sales conversion.

DIAMOND RULE BEHAVIOR

The Diamond Rule is the most advanced approach for working effectively with other people. As a combination of the Golden Rule and the Platinum Rule, it requires you to consider and satisfy your own instinctive concerns and needs while simultaneously addressing the needs of others. Although it takes keen awareness and presence to pull this off, it is truly the "Holy Grail" of human dynamics.

Diamond Rule behavior means effectively managing your identity (personal brand) with others even when your biology (survival response to pressure) is getting triggered (feeling under attack) in the game of business. This is the high-level business relationship game that leads to success. It's rarefied air— a diamond-level play.

When you adhere to the Diamond Rule, you rise above the pressure system, reaching an elevation that makes it easy to focus on solving client problems and reducing the pressure they feel. This makes you stand out as unique and better in the eyes of your client, dramatically increasing your ability to win business.

OUR BRAIN AND PRESSURE

The human brain is the most powerful processor on the planet. It's responsible for incredible advances in art, culture, and technology. Yet, at times it can cause us to act like anything but a human being.

When humans are exposed to a high-enough level of pressure—for instance, when you find yourself in a tense negotiation with a client— the human brain loses its ability to distinguish between actual and perceived risk. This causes the amygdala to kick into high gear to protect you from an impending (though non-life threatening) situation that it fears may kill you.

OVERCOMING BIOLOGY

If you ever find yourself in a life-or-death situation, you will find that your innate reactions represent your greatest chance for survival. It is in these (hopefully rare) moments when you can truly appreciate the natural wisdom of your behavioral style and its ability to keep you alive.

To effectively apply the Diamond Rule, you must recognize the role that pressure and biology play in your life. The only way out is awareness. Awareness will NOT make your biology go away, as it is part of a billion-year-old imperative for survival. Believe us, as long as you're breathing, your biology is not going anywhere.

Instead, we are suggesting that you learn to behave in ways that are counter to what your biology wants you to do. And do so by making better choices. Applying the Diamond Rule means keeping your wits about you, focusing on the other person, and not succumbing to the pressure. To quote legendary football coach Lou Holtz, "Only the unprepared are overcome by pressure."

A BETTER WAY

Let's focus on the two primary skills you'll need to employ the Diamond Rule:

1. *Learning how to manage your own behavior under pressure*

   Before you will ever be able to relate better to others, it's important to look in the mirror and be able to manage your own reactions to pressure.

2. *Increasing your focus on the concerns of others*

When you learn what causes other people to feel stress, you can help reduce their pressure and instantly improve your identity along the way.

Improving and combining these two skills will improve your reputation, advance your career, and create success in the game of business.

SEEING THINGS DIFFERENTLY

In 1985, a 17-year-old Boris Becker rocked the tennis world. The unseeded German bested South African Kevin Curran in four sets to win Wimbledon. The tall, fiery, red-haired player boasted a cannon for a serve. He became the youngest man ever to win a Grand Slam title.

One year later, Andre Agassi would also, like Becker, quit school in the 10th grade to play tennis professionally. In the summer of 1986, Agassi would make his splash in men's tennis. The Las Vegas native brought a lethal forehand, rockstar hair, and a flamboyant fashion style that turned heads. Within 18 months, Agassi would be closing in on a Top 10 ranking.

In 1988 and 1989, Becker and Agassi would meet three times on the court. Each time Becker dominated Agassi, winning easily in straight sets with his powerful serve—a serve Agassi described as "the likes of which the game had never seen before." The third consecutive loss was a 6-1, 6-3 drubbing at Madison Square Garden.

Looking to solve the problem and reverse course, a frustrated Agassi began to watch tapes of Becker.

He paid attention to his serving motion. It paid off as Agassi noticed a small tick. Just before Becker tossed the ball he would stick his tongue out. His tongue would either be in the middle of his lip or

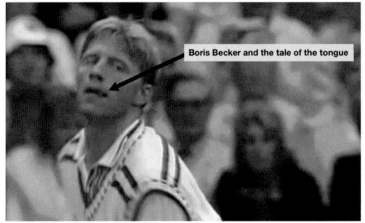

Boris Becker and the tale of the tongue

Photo Credit: YouTube

the left corner of his mouth. The position of his tongue would indicate where the ball was going. When standing to right and serving to the left deuce court, the tongue in the left corner would indicate a wide serve. His tongue in the middle of his mouth was a serve down the middle or into the body.

Agassi would use this insight in his next match against Becker just four months later in Indian Wells, California. It worked brilliantly. He beat Becker handily 6-4, 6-1 in the semifinals. This small insight allowed Andre to react faster and position himself in the right place at critical pressure-filled points in the match. According to Agassi, "the hardest part wasn't returning his serve… the hardest part was not letting him know that I knew this… I would choose the moments where I would use that information on a given point to execute a shot that would break the match wide open."

Over the next nine years, the pair would square off another 10 times. Agassi would win nine of those 10 matches.

The Agassi/Becker story is an apt metaphor for Diamond Goldfish. If you can see business through a new lens as the ultimate game, you can wire yourself for winning. In the words of Marcel Proust, "The voyage of discovery is not in seeking new landscapes, but in having new eyes." Diamond Goldfish challenges you to see sales and the process of developing relationships in a new way. It provides a complete business execution system for generating prosperity and winning in business.

This business execution system is called Market Force®. Market Force is a scientifically-based system with proven effectiveness in the marketplace for over four decades. It is used by leading brands. A partial client list includes Starbucks, Colliers International, Microsoft, WeWork, Alaska Airlines, CBRE, Emaar, AT&T, Savers, and American Pacific Mortgage. These companies leverage the system and its practical tools to power sales and strengthen key relationships in business.

MEETING TRAVIS AND TONY

Travis Carson is the founder of Market Force Global. I met Travis back in 2009. We shared a common friend. Ted Curtin had met Travis at the Ironman Triathlon in Lake Placid while they were both competing. Upon learning about Travis's background as a fellow tennis player, a JD/MBA, and a business thought leader, Ted made the introduction to connect us.

Travis and I bonded immediately. I'll never forget the metaphor that Travis used to describe the power of Market Force. He likened the system to looking for seams on a tennis ball as opposed to looking at the ball itself. This would enable a player to more quickly determine the spin coming off of their opponent's racquet. The ability to quickly discern the amount of slice, topspin, or kick on the ball was significant. A split-second could be the difference between being on your heels and out of position to stepping in to hit a winner. Over the next two years, I'd see first-hand the effectiveness of Market Force while working at Synergy. We'd land our biggest account and increase our sales by 125 percent by using the Market Force sales system.

Nearly a decade later, Travis and I would reconnect. I would meet Tony Cooper, CEO of Market Force. Tony is an accomplished serial entrepreneur who is passionate about bringing out the best in others. Soon the three of us would embark on the first sales/client management book in the Goldfish Series.

Diamond Goldfish uncovers how business is a game. The key to winning in sales is managing relationships and minimizing pressure. Performing at the highest level goes beyond simply treating the prospect the way they prefer to be treated. *Diamond Goldfish* provides perspective and tools for winning in the game of business.

UNDERSTANDING THE FOUR BEHAVIORAL STYLES

Casey, Izzy, Peyton, and Avery. Let's meet the four personas for each of the four behavioral styles:

Casey
Casey is a hard-charging thinker who usually sits in the front of the room. Typically well dressed and image-conscious, Casey wants to accomplish big things and can come across as assertive, maybe even pushy, about their ideas. Casey loves to strategize and craves **control**.

Izzy
Izzy is a people person, a facilitator, who gravitates toward connecting with others and ideas. Izzy is typically loaded with possibilities about everything and appears to think quickly on their feet. Izzy lives "in the now," craves action, and seeks to **influence** others.

Peyton
Peyton is a workhorse who is engrossed in work and thrives on to-do lists. Peyton likes sticking to the plan and will power through almost anything to achieve desired results. Peyton's goal is to produce large volumes of work and **power** through it quickly!

Avery

Avery is an analyzer who loves to focus on gathering information to get into the details. Avery lives in the past and wants to get everything exactly right—all of the time. They feel like they need to become an **authority** on a particular topic before pushing forward with a decision.

Casey, Izzy, Peyton, and Avery represent the four Behavioral Styles. Casey is a Control, Izzy is an Influence, Peyton is a Power, and Avery is an Authority.

WHAT'S YOUR BEHAVIORAL STYLE?

You should be thinking, "Which Style is most like me?" Honestly, that's the price of admission. There is no rank order, no best Style, none of that! Just by knowing what your style is, you can overcome it and begin applying the Diamond Rule to your relationships.

Now let's determine *your* style! Are you a Control, Influence, Power, or Authority? Go to http://diamondgoldfish.com to take the Market Force Styles Indicator Assessment.

Note: You'll need to grab this 8-digit code to access your complimentary assessment.

PN3FM8YK

Once we know our own style, we can begin to look at the life cycle of "selling to" and "working with" others. The sales life cycle is broken down into six primary actions:

1. Reminding yourself of the other person's perspective before you meet with them — setting the foundation for success.

2. Thinking about how you can make a great first impression on the other person when you factor in their Style.

3. Coming up with effective ways for working the sale, including tips on handling negotiations and creating a win-win closing for your potential clients.

4. Considering how to better manage the relationship post-closing, including what to do if a breakdown occurs.

5. Examining ways to acknowledge success once you deliver on what was promised.

6. Focusing on things you can do to solidify your relationship with the other person after your work with them is complete in order to set up for the next go-around.

DIAMOND RULE MATRIX

The Diamond Rule Matrix provides an "at a glance reference tool" for each style and six primary actions.

HOW TO USE THE MATRIX:

Find your style across over the next four pages. Then scroll down to find the style of the person you are working with or selling to. Within each box, you'll find tips on how to put the Diamond Rule into action.

YOUR STYLE

THEIR STYLE

	DIAMOND APPROACH	CONTROL
CONTROL	*MANAGE YOUR BIOLOGY*	**MINDSET:** *Think more about how to help them* **NEUTRALIZE:** *Don't fight their ideas*
	EMPATHIZE WITH THEM	**FOUNDATION:** Prepare to be a Power **FIRST MEETING:** Let them drive **NEGOTIATING:** Tie outcomes to their ideas **ACKNOWLEDGING:** Great idea! **FOLLOWING UP:** Your team was outstanding!
INFLUENCE	*MANAGE YOUR BIOLOGY*	**MINDSET:** *Focus on being more personable* **NEUTRALIZE:** *Being too direct or pushy*
	EMPATHIZE WITH THEM	**FOUNDATION:** Focus on sincerity vs. competence **FIRST MEETING:** Discuss people they know **NEGOTIATING:** Listen and make process **ACKNOWLEDGING:** Enjoyed working with you! **FOLLOWING UP:** Let's meet up for lunch
POWER	*MANAGE YOUR BIOLOGY*	**MINDSET:** *Zero in on tactics and be pragmatic* **NEUTRALIZE:** *Focusing only on big picture*
	EMPATHIZE WITH THEM	**FOUNDATION:** Be cordial and avoid being pushy **FIRST MEETING:** Come across as a hard worker **NEGOTIATING:** Be collaborative not just 1-sided **ACKNOWLEDGING:** We make a great team! **FOLLOWING UP:** What can I do next for you?
AUTHORITY	*MANAGE YOUR BIOLOGY*	**MINDSET:** *Be interested in historical context* **NEUTRALIZE:** *Talking too much about the future*
	EMPATHIZE WITH THEM	**FOUNDATION:** Prepare to listen to their concerns **FIRST MEETING:** Let them discuss obstacles **NEGOTIATING:** Slow down & talk through points **ACKNOWLEDGING:** Your insights were a lifesaver! **FOLLOWING UP:** Let's do a project retrospective

YOUR STYLE

	DIAMOND APPROACH	INFLUENCE
CONTROL	MANAGE YOUR BIOLOGY	**MINDSET:** Be on point & more business focused **NEUTRALIZE:** Instinct to "just wing it"
	EMPATHIZE WITH THEM	**FOUNDATION:** Prepare with crisp approach **FIRST MEETING:** Focus on their business point **NEGOTIATING:** Be more formal than informal **ACKNOWLEDGING:** Great strategy for us to follow! **FOLLOWING UP:** Where's the next challenge?
INFLUENCE	MANAGE YOUR BIOLOGY	**MINDSET:** Be social AND help with structure **NEUTRALIZE:** Temptation not to do business
	EMPATHIZE WITH THEM	**FOUNDATION:** Don't just create a friend **FIRST MEETING:** Have fun but don't compete **NEGOTIATING:** Keep it light, but capture details **ACKNOWLEDGING:** Let's go celebrate! **FOLLOWING UP:** Let's have some more fun
POWER	MANAGE YOUR BIOLOGY	**MINDSET:** Avoid being unorganized **NEUTRALIZE:** Over-emphasis on sincerity
	EMPATHIZE WITH THEM	**FOUNDATION:** Prepare to be more like a Power **FIRST MEETING:** Get invested in their projects **NEGOTIATING:** Go point by point, work together **ACKNOWLEDGING:** I love working with you! **FOLLOWING UP:** How can I help you further?
AUTHORITY	MANAGE YOUR BIOLOGY	**MINDSET:** One thought and one step at a time **NEUTRALIZE:** Careful not to come across chaotic
	EMPATHIZE WITH THEM	**FOUNDATION:** Act more like an Authority **FIRST MEETING:** Be patient, listen, & don't just talk **NEGOTIATING:** Have grounding for your positions **ACKNOWLEDGING:** Thank you for having my back! **FOLLOWING UP:** Here's a gift certificate for you

THEIR STYLE

YOUR STYLE

THEIR STYLE	DIAMOND APPROACH	POWER
CONTROL	*MANAGE YOUR BIOLOGY*	**MINDSET:** *Be organized and focused on priorities* **NEUTRALIZE:** *Coming across as too busy to implement*
	EMPATHIZE WITH THEM	**FOUNDATION:** Focus on high level objectives, not tactics **FIRST MEETING:** Show ability to think strategically **NEGOTIATING:** Appeal to their image throughout **ACKNOWLEDGING:** Your direction kept me on point! **FOLLOWING UP:** What is the next mountain to climb?
INFLUENCE	*MANAGE YOUR BIOLOGY*	**MINDSET:** *Be open to brainstorming* **NEUTRALIZE:** *Need to leave with a checklist too quickly*
	EMPATHIZE WITH THEM	**FOUNDATION:** Relax at the beginning & bring structure **FIRST MEETING:** Don't impose too much structure **NEGOTIATING:** Be patient, let them go first **ACKNOWLEDGING:** I appreciated your high energy! **FOLLOWING UP:** Here's a plaque for your great work
POWER	*MANAGE YOUR BIOLOGY*	**MINDSET:** *Create a partner and focus on being a Control* **NEUTRALIZE:** *Temptation of only focusing tactically*
	EMPATHIZE WITH THEM	**FOUNDATION:** Show loyalty early and often **FIRST MEETING:** Compare lists and adhere to theirs **NEGOTIATING:** Work toward a presumptive next step **ACKNOWLEDGING:** We are a powehouse team! **FOLLOWING UP:** What's our next to-do together?
AUTHORITY	*MANAGE YOUR BIOLOGY*	**MINDSET:** *Focus on quality over volume* **NEUTRALIZE:** *Rushing any one direction without thinking*
	EMPATHIZE WITH THEM	**FOUNDATION:** Prepare your resume and credentials **FIRST MEETING:** Show you are thinking about priorities **NEGOTIATING:** Be exacting & focus on quality over cost **ACKNOWLEDGING:** I appreciate your detailed approach! **FOLLOWING UP:** Here are my thoughts on what worked

THEIR STYLE

	DIAMOND APPROACH	AUTHORITY
CONTROL	MANAGE YOUR BIOLOGY	**MINDSET:** *Be open to new ideas and new possibilites* **NEUTRALIZE:** *Too much focus on reasons why not*
	EMPATHIZE WITH THEM	**FOUNDATION:** Demonstrate you get their ideas **FIRST MEETING:** Be interested in their love for the future **NEGOTIATING:** Be passionate in the process **ACKNOWLEDGING:** You showed me what's possible! **FOLLOWING UP:** Can we brainstorm about the future?
INFLUENCE	MANAGE YOUR BIOLOGY	**MINDSET:** *Be authentically interested in them* **NEUTRALIZE:** *Focus on numbers and details*
	EMPATHIZE WITH THEM	**FOUNDATION:** Prepare to go faster than feels natural **FIRST MEETING:** Avoid slowing down their process **NEGOTIATING:** Don't argue all points, pick your battles **ACKNOWLEDGING:** You made this project fun! **FOLLOWING UP:** Can I buy you dinner?
POWER	MANAGE YOUR BIOLOGY	**MINDSET:** *Bring a bias for action & getting down to business* **NEUTRALIZE:** *Coming across as negative on past work*
	EMPATHIZE WITH THEM	**FOUNDATION:** Create a checklist of discussion topics **FIRST MEETING:** Move with pace over precision focus **NEGOTIATING:** Avoid being rude or pushy **ACKNOWLEDGING:** You've done great work! **FOLLOWING UP:** Can we do more great work together?
AUTHORITY	MANAGE YOUR BIOLOGY	**MINDSET:** *Discuss the past but focus on the future* **NEUTRALIZE:** *Comfort level of not making an decisions*
	EMPATHIZE WITH THEM	**FOUNDATION:** Avoid analysis paralysis **FIRST MEETING:** Let them talk, then act like a Control **NEGOTIATING:** Don't wait forever; walk away if need be **ACKNOWLEDGING:** Your analysis was key at every step! **FOLLOWING UP:** I created this deal review for you

M.I.N.E. FOR DIAMONDS

Remember, diamonds aren't just lying around ready to be picked up. You have to go searching for them. Our M.I.N.E. approach will best prepare you to apply the Diamond Rule.

Here are the four questions when mining for Diamonds:

[Mindset] What Style am I dealing with?

[Identify] What is the situation?

[Neutralize] What do I need to do to set aside my Style? Before you will ever be able to relate better with others, it's important to look in the mirror and neutralize your own reactions to pressure. The dictionary definition of neutralize is "to render (something) harmless by applying an opposite force or effect."

[Empathize] What am I doing to address their needs? Being empathetic means increasing your focus on the concerns of others. When you learn what causes other people to feel stress, you can help reduce their pressure and instantly improve your identity along the way.

THE THREE KEYS TO SUCCESS

There are only three ways to achieve success with the Diamond Rule—APPLY, APPLY, and APPLY. In the words of Rob Hill, Sr. "Knowledge without application is a waste. Those who just "know" will always come in second to those who "do." Put what you know in motion… apply what you've learned."

Once you manage pressure, the next focus is communication.

CHAPTER 15

WHY SILVER?

"There are only two types of speakers in this world.
The nervous . . . and the liars."

- Mark Twain

Silver became the 10th color in the Goldfish Series in 2020.

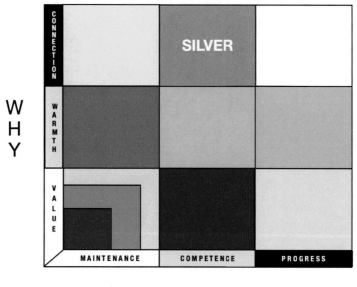

Why silver for communication? There are two reasons for the second metal in the Goldfish Series. They are readability and conductivity. Let's examine each:

READABILITY

Readability was inspired by my late father. Nicknamed the "Silver Fox," John Phelps Sr. enlisted in the United States Army Air Force at the age of 17. After finishing basic training in early 1948, he was sent to school in Fort Monmouth, New Jersey. My Dad would become a member of the United States Signal Corps.

John graduated from Signal Corps school and became a radio repairman stationed at Hickam Air Force Base in Hawaii. The base in Oahu was next to Pearl Harbor. As a repairman, one of his main jobs was to test the strength and readability of radio signals. Specifically, they were judging volume and clarity.

A signal strength and readability report is a standardized format for reporting the strength of a radio signal and the readability of a signal transmitted by another station.

The scale was from 1-5. The number one represented the worst and five was the best. The first number in the scale represented the signal strength and the second number represented the signal clarity. If both strength (volume) and clarity were excellent, the receiver would reply "five by five." That was shorthand for "I understand you perfectly." We reference this scale today when we say "loud and clear." The five-by-five framework is ideally suited for presenting. Our goal when presenting is to come across "Loud" and "Clear."

CONDUCTIVITY

The second reason for choosing silver to represent presentation communication is its conductivity. Silver exhibits the highest electrical conductivity and thermal conductivity of any metal.

Why do we think conductivity matters? When communicating, you are the conduit between the information and the audience. Your goal is to allow that information to be transferred in the best possible way. You as the presenter are responsible for creating the connection.

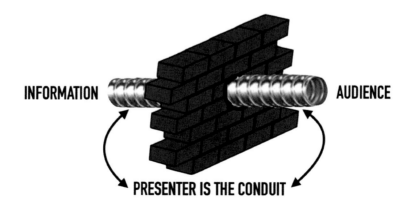

INFORMATION   AUDIENCE

PRESENTER IS THE CONDUIT

OUR BIGGEST FEAR

What's the most common fear for humans? It's speaking. According to *Forbes*, "The fear of public speaking is the most common fear and prevents many people from achieving their potential." A shocking 74 percent of Americans have fears and anxiety toward public speaking.

Our number two fear—dying.

Does this make any sense? We, as humans, have so lost perspective that when asked what we fear the most, we will choose a threat to our identity over actual death! In the brilliant words of comedian Jerry Seinfeld, "For the average person, if you have to be at a funeral, you would rather be in the casket than doing the eulogy."

The fear of speaking and presenting is called glossophobia. Some may feel a slight nervousness at the thought of public speaking, while others experience full-on panic and fear.

Why? Because our brain has a hard time distinguishing between actual risk (loss of life) and perceived risk (threat to our identity). Our brains are wired to respond to threats in a particular way—regardless of the actual threat.

To my knowledge, no one has literally died giving a presentation. But think about what happens when you stand up or sit down to present. Your brain goes into threat mode. Your amygdala senses a threat and sends signals to your limbic system. The limbic system effectively shuts down your neocortex, the thinking part of your brain. It then releases chemicals that increase your heart rate, breathing rate, and sweat gland activity.

And to be candid, even for an experienced presenter, these feelings of nervousness and excitement never completely go away. You can't unwire or unlearn biology. Mark Twain made light of this when he said, "There are only two types of speakers in this world. The nervous . . . and the liars."

Overcoming these feelings and becoming great at communicating is the focus of *Silver Goldfish*.

BIGGEST MYTH OF COMMUNICATION

You just finished a business presentation. Perhaps it was a sales pitch, a conference presentation, or a divisional update. People nodded as you finished. Some may have come up and congratulated you on the pitch, update, or talk, so you're feeling good. You're convinced you did a good job communicating your message and you're ready to see what big thing happens next.

But let's assess the situation. How can you tell if the desired communication has taken place? You can do so by answering these three questions:

- Can your audience recall the central message, your One Thing?
- Are they able to apply the message to their lives?
- Did they understand the call to action and know what to do next?

Here's the probable reality. If you are like most presenters, you likely missed the mark. You bought into the myth. In the words of George Bernard Shaw, "The single biggest problem in communication is the illusion that it has taken place."

The fact that you might be an ineffective presenter is most likely not your fault. You probably are emulating the hundreds, if not thousands, of presentations you've seen.

"What's your definition of COMMUNICATION success?" It's difficult to nail down. Here's a simple definition we've settled on:

Communication occurs when the AUDIENCE can repeat your message in their language.

The people who can tell you if communication happened are the most important people in the room: your audience. Right now, they're not here to ask. So let's figure out some little things that will make a constructive difference in your presentations.

In summary, the goldfish in *Silver Goldfish* represents differentiation. How do you stand out by doing the little things that improve your ability as a presenter? And the silver in *Silver Goldfish* symbolizes how well you rise above the noise and clarify your message. How you become the conduit for your message to come across "Loud" and "Clear."

Now, let's examine the 10 keys to being loud and clear.

10 KEYS TO BEING LOUD & CLEAR

There are 10 keys to effective communication. There are five keys for volume and five keys for clarity for improving your presentations. We'll provide a TIP for each of the keys.

For background, the precise origin of the word TIP is uncertain. It is commonly traced to coffeehouses in seventeenth-century England. The word "tips" was first used for gratuities. A jar with a sign reading, "To Insure Prompt Service" sat on the counter. You put a coin in the jar to be served quickly.

We adopted a different acronym for the word:

> **T**O
>
> **I**MPROVE
>
> **P**RESENTATION
>
> **S**KILLS

Here are tips on how to be heard "Loud" and "Clear" when presenting.

Loud refers to the ability to be heard above distractions.

1. **Impress** - The first impression you create is extremely important when it comes to presenting.

TIP - The standard should be to dress appropriately and stylishly for the audience to make a positive first impression.

2. **Connect** - Great speakers connect with their audiences. They understand a simple truth: The audience wants you to succeed. They don't require you to be perfect. In the words of speaking coach Stephanie Scotti, "It's not about perfection when presenting; it's about connection."

TIP - S.T.O.P. This acronym is one of the best speaking techniques for establishing connection. You deliver a **S**ingle **T**hought to **O**ne **P**erson. You think of and compose your next thought while finding a new person in the audience. You are not allowed to start delivering the thought until you establish eye contact. Then you deliver that next single thought. Lather, rinse, repeat.

3. **Express** - Part of being heard above the din of distraction is the skill of expressing yourself.

TIP - Go bigger with your voice. As with most things in life, if it doesn't scare you a bit, you are not going big enough.

4. **Facilitate** - You need to make it easy for them to pay attention. That's the definition of facilitate: to make easier; to help bring about.

TIP – When dealing with a distraction, either fix it, feature it, or forget it.

5. **Entertain** - The definition of entertain, according to *Webster*, is to hold the attention of agreeably, to admit into the mind; consider. That's the real goal of a presenter—to get the audience to consider their points and claims.

TIP – Variety is key to keeping the attention of the audience. Mix it up every 8 to 10 minutes.

We've examined the five key elements of being LOUD and heard above distractions. Next, we'll examine the five key elements of CLEAR.

Clear refers to the clarity of your message.

1. **Objective** - Probably the greatest problem with clarity in business presentations is the tendency to try to put too much into the presentation.

TIP - We need to release ourselves of the obligation to cover everything we know. Figure out what is important to the audience. Find out your reason for being on that stage giving that presentation. Know your objective.

2. **Simplify** - The first step in helping your audience understand is to figure out your "One Thing."

TIP – Avoid the curse of knowledge. Find the "One Thing," the central idea for your entire presentation.

3. **Outline** – This is a time of exploration. It includes understanding your audience and coming up with the structure of your presentation.

TIP – How many main points will you cover? Is there a magic number when presenting? Yes, there is—it's three. Three is the magic number. And when it comes to presenting, it's even more important. If the goal when speaking is to be remember-able, then you need to take advantage of this powerful heuristic.

4. **Visualize** - What's the best way to make your presentation memorable? The answer will frequently involve visuals. These visuals can take the shape of slides, whiteboards, flipcharts, or props.

TIP – Leverage the picture superiority effect. Using images can enhance your audience's ability to remember your message or call to action. Pictures and images are more likely to be remembered than words alone.

5. **Time** – You need to manage your time when presenting. How long should your presentation be? Let's look for inspiration from the late Franklin Delano Roosevelt. He said, "Be sincere. Be brief. Be seated."

TIP – Time is precious. Curate it carefully. Always end on time. It's the cardinal rule of presenting.

No one reading this was born speaking. Not one of us. And we certainly weren't born speaking well. It's a skill, not a talent.

Your audience has plenty to occupy their minds; you need to be louder. Your audience won't retain nearly as much as you think they should; you need to be clearer.

Success in presenting is that the audience can repeat your message. That's a tall order with so much information swirling in our lives. Find a way to help them remember your message.

Silver represents the 10th color in the Series. Now, let's look at Black again.

CHAPTER 16

WHY BLACK, PART DEUX?

*"I've been 40 years discovering that the queen of
all colors was black."*

- Pierre-Auguste Renoir

Getting to the color black at the top right of the matrix is the pinnacle for any brand. This means you have graduated through all of the previous colors.

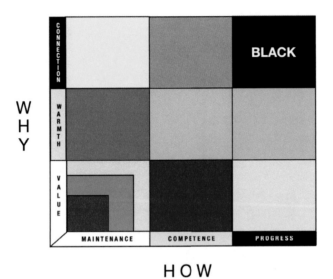

This is similar to martial arts where attaining a Black Belt represents the most prestigious stage of learning. To obtain a black belt, a student must have full control of his or her abilities and knowledge. Those with a black belt also possess the power to teach what they've learned to new students. Our progression to black has gone purple, green, gold, blue, red, pink, yellow, gray, diamond, and silver. In martial arts, the progression is typically white, gray, yellow, orange, green, blue, purple, brown, and then black.

BEING IN THE BLACK

The expression "in the black" has a positive connotation. It is used to refer to profitability and current financial health. A company is said to be in the black if it is profitable or, more specifically, if the company produces positive earnings after accounting for all expenses.

The term has roots when accountants updated financial data by hand before computers. Accountants used different colored ink—both black and red—in their book to denote a company's profitability. If you had negative earnings, red ink meant you were "in the red." Today, negative numbers are typically entered in parenthesis or with a minus sign.

It is better to consistently be in the black than in the red as this indicates solid business performance. It indicates the ability to:

- pay down debt and maintain their cash flow during difficult times

- answer to their directors

- pay dividends to their shareholders

- raise capital for any financial needs

Black is the combination of all colors. Next, let's wrap things up with the I.D.E.A. framework and final words.

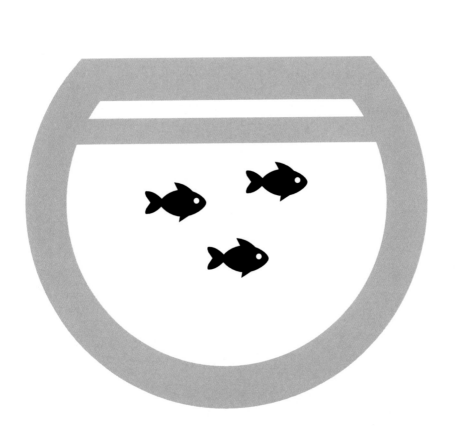

SECTION III

THE HOW?

CHAPTER 17

THE I.D.E.A. FRAMEWORK

"Ideas without action are worthless."

— Harvey Mackay

Since the release of *Purple Goldfish* in 2012, I've had the opportunity to train hundreds of companies on the various colors in the Series. As you might imagine, it's not enough to help an organization understand the concept of a Goldfish and why they need them. Organizations also need help creating their own initiatives. To help with the creation process, we put together the I.D.E.A. framework.

Here's the overview of the I.D.E.A. framework:

It is a 12-step framework for identifying and implementing a Goldfish Strategy in your organization.

INQUIRE – understand what is important and what opportunities exist in your current customer or employee journey.

- Step One: Gather insight
- Step Two: Create journey maps
- Step Three: Identify gaps or opportunities

DESIGN – With insights, you can now set your focus on generating ideas. Ideas that address the gaps or opportunities in your current customer or employee journeys.

- Step One: Set your focus

- Step Two: Ask big questions

- Step Three: Organize your ideas

EVALUATE – complete internal and external analysis on the feasibility of your ideas and determine which Goldfish to try out.

- Step One: Internal evaluation

- Step Two: External validation

- Step Three: Pilot

ADVANCE – implement widespread rollout and measure the results

- Step One: Achieve buy-in internally

- Step Two: Roll out the experience

- Step Three: Set up a feedback loop with continuous measurement

CHAPTER 18

FINAL WORDS

"I wish someone would have told me that this life is ours to choose. No one's handing you the keys or a book with all the rules. The little that I know I'll tell to you."

– P!NK, from the song,
"All I Know So Far"

"So long and thanks for all the fish!"

- Douglas Adams, from the book,
Hitchhiker's Guide to the Galaxy

Here is the final word ... or words of *Black Goldfish*.

Finishing a book with the right word or set of words is paramount.

In the words of Mark Twain, "The difference between the almost right word and the right word is really a large matter. 'tis the difference between the lightning bug and the lightning."

Look no further than the words spoken by President Franklin Delano Roosevelt in a joint address to Congress.

FDR realized that words matter. His close adviser, Harry Hopkins, recalled the scene in his personal diary after the attack at Pearl Harbor:

> There was some discussion about the President's message to Congress. The President expressed himself very strongly that he was going to submit a precise message. [Secretary of State Cordell] Hull urged very strongly that the President review the whole history of the Japanese relations in a strong document that might take half an hour to read. The President objected.

FDR wanted to be loud and clear. The first sentence of the speech needed punch. The original draft was, "a date which will live in **world history**."

Instead, FDR addressed Congress with "YESTERDAY, December 7, 1941, _ a date which will live in **infamy** the United States of America was suddenly and deliberately attacked by naval and air forces of the Empire of Japan."

White House speechwriter Sarada Peri shared with *The Washington Post,*

If you think about that word choice change... it's not just a rhetorical flourish... It gives greater meaning. He is making a judgment call about what this moment is. It is an act that is treacherous and requires some kind of response, and it's part of what speech writing is about, which is clarifying to the point of finding the right word.

FDR's "infamy" speech which was recommended to be 30 minutes... came in at just over six minutes. Within an hour every member of Congress, except for one, voted to declare war.

THE RIGHT WORDS

When have you used the right word or developed the right word or words?

I think of the words I've used in the Goldfish Series to represent some important ideas. Words such as:

- LAGNIAPPE - the little things that are thrown in for good measure for customers and employees

- ATTABOYS - little things you do to recognize your employees

- VITAL FEW - the idea that you don't treat all customers and employees the same

- INFO-SENSE - using data to really understand customers and personalize their experience

- FOR-PURPOSE - the idea that tax filing status will become negligible in the future... that companies will only be seen as for-purpose or not-for-purpose

- FLAWSOME - that our flaws hold the key to what makes us awesome

- GEZELLIG - little things that create happiness and a distinct feeling of connection

- MANAGE THE GRAY - the need to lead across five generations in the workplace

- DIAMOND RULE - the ability to manage ourselves and others under pressure

- 5 BY 5 - the need to focus on being "loud and clear" when communicating

I want to finish *Black Goldfish* with these final words:

> Your brand today is no longer what you tell people it is.
>
> It is the differentiated experience your employees deliver.
>
> It is what you stand for and how your customers feel about you.
>
> And most importantly, your brand is what your customers and employees tell others about their experience.
>
> All else is derivative of this and only this.

To quote Alecia Beth Moore, "That's all I know, that's all I know so far."

ABOUT THE AUTHOR

STAN PHELPS, CSP

Stan Phelps is a best-selling author, keynote speaker, and workshop facilitator. He believes that today's organizations must focus on meaningful differentiation to create experiences that win the hearts of both employees and customers.

He is the founder of StanPhelpsSpeaks.com. Stan offers keynotes, workshops, and Goldfish Tank programs that are designed to drive loyalty and sales. He helps organizations connect with the hearts and minds of customers and employees.

Prior to professional speaking, Stan had a 20-year career in marketing that included leadership positions at IMG, adidas, PGA Exhibitions, and Synergy. At Synergy, he worked on award-winning experiential programs for top brands such as KFC, Wachovia, NASCAR, Starbucks, and M&M's.

Stan is a TEDx speaker, an IBM Futurist, and a Certified Speaking Professional. His writing has been syndicated on top sites such as *Forbes, Customer Think, and Business2Community*. He has spoken at more than 500 events across Australia, Bahrain, Canada, Ecuador, France, Germany, Holland, Israel, Japan, Malaysia, Peru, Russia, Singapore, Spain, Sweden, the UK, and the US.

He is the author of the Goldfish Series of business books:

- *Purple Goldfish 2.0 - 10 Ways to Attract Raving Customers*
- *Green Goldfish 2.0 - 15 Keys to Driving Employee Engagement*

- *Golden Goldfish - The Vital Few*

- *Blue Goldfish - Using Technology, Data, and Analytics to Drive Both Profits and Prophets*

- *Purple Goldfish Service Edition - 12 Ways Hotels, Restaurants, and Airlines Win the Right Customers*

- *Red Goldfish - Motivating Sales and Loyalty Through Shared Passion and Purpose*

- *Pink Goldfish - Defy Normal, Exploit Imperfection, and Captivate Your Customers*

- *Purple Goldfish Franchise Edition - The Ultimate S.Y.S.T.E.M. for Franchisors and Franchisees*

- *Yellow Goldfish - Nine Ways to Drive Happiness in Business for Growth, Productivity, and Prosperity*

- *Gray Goldfish - Navigating the Gray Areas to Successfully Lead Every Generation*

- *Red Goldfish Nonprofit Edition - How the Best Nonprofits Leverage Their Purpose to Increase Engagement and Impact*

- *Red Goldfish Promo Edition - How Promotional Products Leverage Purpose to Increase Impact*

- *Diamond Goldfish - Excel Under Pressure & Thrive in the Game of Business*

- *Silver Goldfish - Loud & Clear: The 10 Keys to Delivering Memorable Business Presentations*

and one fun book...

Bar Tricks, Bad Jokes, & Even Worse Stories

Stan received a BS in Marketing and Human Resources from Marist College, a JD/MBA from Villanova University, and a certificate for

Achieving Breakthrough Service from Harvard Business School. He is a Certified Net Promoter Associate, an Instructor at the ANA School of Marketing, and has taught as an adjunct professor of marketing at New York University, Rutgers University, and Manhattanville College.

Stan lives in Cary, North Carolina, with his wife, Jennifer, and their two boys, Thomas and James.

To book Stan for an upcoming keynote, webinar, virtual talk, workshop, or Goldfish Tank program go to stanphelpsspeaks.com. You can reach Stan at stan@purplegoldfish.com, call +1.919.360.4702, or connect with him on Linkedin: https://linkedin.com/in/StanPhelps